The most revolutionary measure

A history of the
Rural Development Commission
1909-1999

Alan Rogers

ISBN 1 869964 71 3

First published in February 1999

Published by the Rural Development Commission⋆
141 Castle Street, Salisbury, Wiltshire, SP1 3TP England

A CIP catalogue record for this book is available from the British Library

Designed by Fox Design Consultants
Printed in England by Battley Brothers Printers Limited

⋆ 1 April 1999 marks another chapter in the Rural Development Commission's long history, when the newly-established Regional Development Agencies in England take over responsibility for the Commission's rural regeneration work in the regions and the remainder of the Commission's activities - its national advisory role and countrywide work - are merged with those of the Countryside Commission to form the new Countryside Agency.

Contents

Foreword by Lord Shuttleworth

For those involved in the development and implementation of rural policy, the fascination of Dr Rogers' story spanning some ninety years will be his identification of consistent threads throughout the life of the Rural Development Commission, some of which still run on. For others, perhaps with a general interest if no direct experience in rural policy, it may be the irony in Alan Rogers' tale which strikes more forcibly, as he demonstrates how a dynamic organisation comes to an end just when it seems to have acquired the status and executive ability which was missing in its early years. In providing a comprehensive and much needed history of the Commission, Dr Rogers subtly points to a number of issues which need further debate and resolution as we enter an uncharted phase of public administration of rural policy.

As this book shows, the Rural Development Commission constantly adjusted its activities to meet new circumstances, reflecting the continuous change in economic and social conditions in rural areas. Dr Rogers explains how initial success in agricultural research and education was followed within ten years of the Commission's beginnings by its first steps towards the rural industrial support and rural community development which proved to be central activities throughout its existence. In this process of adjustment, an essential role was always played by Commissioners with relevant experience who were able to guide the organisation by their personal understanding of the rural scene.

Another thread in the story is the Commission's sometimes uneasy relationship with government. Tensions usually exist between those who allocate a budget and those who spend it. Indeed, the Commission itself, in its own relationship with those bodies to whom it gave grants, was not always blameless. However, as Dr Rogers shows, the Commission's difficulties with government went deeper.

As an agency, and not an independent lobby group for the countryside, the Commission was somewhat constrained in overt comment on some important or controversial issues, thereby restricting its opportunity to create a public reputation. On the other hand, governments did not always draw on, or pay much heed to, the expertise and advice available to them privately from the Commission, as for example during the debate on rural depopulation in the 1950s and '60s. This situation, coupled with a tendency for departments to second-guess even quite detailed matters, is a fact of life for most government agencies. In the case of the Commission, however, the frustrations it caused were compounded by periodic challenges from the Treasury and other parts of government to its need to exist. The Commission, with a broad cross-cutting role, was not easily accommodated in a governmental system organised around discrete issues and services. The Commission's greatest successes came about when it brought some focus to its effort to support economic and social initiatives. Loss of jobs from agricultural and other traditional rural industries, together with the need to diversify the employment skills and economic base, were constant concerns over the years and were met with responses tailored to the circumstances. The encouragement of craftsmen in the inter-war years, the enormously successful workshop building programme (started in 1947 but at its height in the 1970s and '80s), the innovative and pioneering response to rural coalfield closures, the recognition of the importance of tourism and the support for the provision of low-cost rural housing are all examples of this.

It was as late as 1975 that a speech by the Commission's then Chairman featured depopulation as a major threat to the countryside. However, by then there were some signs that the population of many rural areas was increasing and, partly as a consequence, signs of the emergence of the most difficult challenge of the '80s and today – the perceived conflict between meeting the needs of the people in the countryside and the aspirations of those who wanted to move to it, and the giving of proper protection to the landscape and natural environment.

The Commission's view was that a strong rural economy was an essential part of a sustainable rural environment. The Commission did not prescribe the nature of that economy, but emphasised that it must be evolutionary and dynamic. As demands for ever-greater environmental protection grew, Commissioners insisted that the needs of people living and working in rural areas were of at least as high a priority, and that ways could be found to address them which would be compatible with, and indeed, integral to a sustainable countryside. They warned against a view of rural England merely as a place for leisure for the urban dweller, or as a dormitory or retirement home for the affluent. Government gave support to the Commission's approach in the 1995 Rural White Paper, a document which may come to be seen as a high-water mark in institutional understanding of the countryside.

Barely two years after that White Paper, a new government was announcing that the Commission's regeneration work would be transferred to eight new regional development agencies and, later, that its remaining national advisory and countryside work would be taken on by another new agency which would also incorporate the Countryside Commission.

The reader may conclude that government's decision was not so much about seeking to better the Commission's impact on rural areas as about fulfilling a different agenda - the introduction of a regional structure for a broad spectrum of policy implementation. Privileged to have been Chairman of the Rural Development Commission for some seven and a half years prior to that, I am sensitive to the risk that the information and statistics about rural matters and the practical experience built up by the Commission and its staff during its long life will be dissipated. However, if full use can be made of the existing expertise, and if the Commission's objectives for the economic and social well-being of rural people are vigorously pursued by the new agencies, then there may yet be more chapters to add to this most readable, useful and timely work by Alan Rogers.

Lord Shuttleworth
Chairman, Rural Development Commission
1990-1997

Preface

This history of the Rural Development Commission was conceived during the writing of a general account of the development of rural planning in England and Wales, which I undertook with my late friend Professor Gordon Cherry of the University of Birmingham. Ever interested in the next thing on the writing stocks, Gordon encouraged me to develop my ideas and to approach the Commission with a view to support for the project. We both agreed that previous accounts of rural planning history had generally ignored the role of the Commission, despite the fact that it had been a continuous presence on the rural development stage for virtually the whole century and had been responsible in one way or another for many important developments over the years.

A second, more personal reason, made me keen to realise this idea. My own institution, Wye College, had been involved with the work of the Development Commission, not least by being in receipt of frequent grants in aid of its work. Moreover, Wye's first Principal, Daniel Hall, had been appointed as one of the first Commissioners in 1910 and was, as much as any man, to have an enormous influence upon its work, not least in the creation of our system of agricultural education and research. One objective of this work is to remind a modern audience of the achievements of someone who was one of the foremost agricultural scientists of this century.

I was fortunate that the idea of a history found favour with the Commission, not least with the then Chief Executive, Richard Butt and the Chairman, Lord Shuttleworth. Historians both, they appreciated the need for a formal record of the Commission's activities over many decades. None of us realised, when the idea was first mooted in August 1994, that this study might prove, in practice, to be a valedictory one. In the later stages of writing this book the Labour government, in pursuance of its proposals to create Regional Development Agencies, signalled its intention to amalgamate the Rural Development Commission with the Countryside Commission and to place some of the Commission's work with the new Agencies. Whatever one's views on regional development, it seems a pity that we shall be cheated of a ninetieth birthday party in 2000.

Above all, this study has been a labour of love and I am very grateful to my family and to colleagues and friends in the Commission and at Wye College for allowing me to undertake its research and writing. In a very real way it has proved a necessary refuge from what that wise observer of the modern university scene, Professor Laurie Taylor, has referred to as 'the diverse forms of madness which have swept over our institutions of higher education' in the last few years.

This is substantially a desk study, based upon the formal records such as the annual reports of the Commission and its agencies, and also the unpublished Minutes and sundry papers available in the Public Record Office. In addition, its production has been made more interesting in two ways. First, I was able to interview several key personalities (see Acknowledgements) who, despite initial protestations as to failing memory, proved to be wonderful sources of insight and information. Second, I was very aware that I had, in a very minor way, been personally involved with the work of the Commission during the last twenty years. Whether this was an advantage or not I do not know. My assessments of situations, especially the activities of the Rural Community Councils and the creation of ACRE, are inevitably coloured by my own involvement.

I have tried to make this study a critical but readable one – and not something overburdened with facts. By the same token, I have consciously avoided footnotes and (breaking the academic habit of a lifetime) text referencing. Some important sources are listed at the end. Inevitably some will think that I have missed out critical events as well as misinterpreting some others. For this I apologise, with the plea that I have attempted a critical account produced by a (near) outsider and that the need to keep the book within reasonable limits has inevitably removed some detail. For those who feel the need for a factual record, I have included a chronology of major events as an Appendix. My main intentions in producing this study have been to set the activities of the Rural Development Commission within the context of the main economic, social and political developments of the times and, thereby, to bring to a wider audience the very important role which the Commission has had in the development of the rural areas of this country. Whether the story has truly justified Keir Hardie's view of the Commission as 'the most revolutionary measure', I leave to the individual reader. Whatever the view, there is no doubt that the rural world would have been different had it never existed.

Alan Rogers
October 1998
Old Wives Lees, Kent

Acknowledgements

Many people have helped with the production of this Report. In particular I would mention:

- Staff in the various libraries which I have used, especially Sian Phelps in the Kempe Centre, Wye College; staff in the former library at the Commission's headquarters in Salisbury; staff at the Public Record Office at Kew.

- Staff and members of the Rural Development Commission. The continued support of Richard Butt, the Chief Executive, and Lord Shuttleworth is mentioned in the Preface. I would also mention the late Brian Baxter for his help in the early stages of the work in Salisbury. My thanks are due to other current and former staff of the Commission for their help, especially Gillian Kempster, Judy Basset and Vivien Moreland. I give a special mention to Margaret Clark whose commitment to the work of the Commission, as judged both by time and effort, is second to none. I gained a great deal of information and insight (and pleasure too) from comprehensive discussions and correspondence with former Commissioners and staff of the Commission and CoSIRA. Specific mention should be made in this regard of Lady Albemarle, Lord Northfield, Lord Vinson, Brian Lincoln, Ken Reeves, Arnold Pentelow and John Williams.

- Particular thanks go to Laura Sessions and Bridget Cue in the Environment Department at Wye College for their sterling efforts in turning my handwriting into suitably word-processed format.

1

A vague and grandiose idea

CHAPTER 1

Origins

On the afternoon of 29 April 1909, the Chancellor of the Exchequer, David Lloyd George, outlined to the House of Commons a varied package of social and economic reforms in his Budget Statement. An integral part of his proposals concerned the creation of a 'development scheme' designed to revive the economy and social life of the rural parts of the United Kingdom. Thus was announced the impending birth of an agency which was to exist for almost nine decades, during which it would make a radical impact on the British countryside and on the lives of its inhabitants.

The origins of the Rural Development Commission lie first in the growing concerns which had developed from the last decades of the nineteenth century regarding the state of the rural economy. The seriousness of the Great Depression is still debated and it seems likely that its effects were exaggerated, not least by contemporary commentators. Certainly some farming areas suffered more than others and arable farmers were harder hit than those with livestock enterprises. Equally, the dereliction of land, the bankruptcies of farmers and the migration of workers to the towns can be seen as a necessary and inevitable restructuring of British agriculture in the face of foreign competition. However, whatever the balance of argument, the perception at the time, and especially by the early years of the twentieth century, was one of rural crisis. The blame was variously put. The influx of cheaper foodstuffs from the Americas and Australia was seen by some as the obvious cause, together with the free trade principles which had allowed it. Others saw the crisis as due to an antiquated structure of rural society and land ownership which was precariously founded upon a high input, high output system of farming which could not compete with the lower costs of foreign producers. Bad weather and poor harvests in the 1870s and 1880s had clearly compounded the problem.

If the Great Depression and its associated rural dereliction set the tone for a radical change, then so also did another aspect of the agriculture of those times. For just as the arable farmers were being bankrupted and land was going into idleness, so at the same time was there innovation and experimentation in farming methods. In dairying and market gardening, for example, farmers with more entrepreneurial flair than their fellows showed that there were ways to farm successfully. And immigrant Scottish farmers were quick to move to easier land in the eastern and southern English counties, where they were able to show their neighbours, through dint of hard work, that a living was still to be had. Moreover, the flaws in the primitive, and often non-existent, systems of cost accounting which British farmers employed were increasingly exposed. Those more modern farmers who developed more sophisticated financial systems were able to control their costs much better and stood more chance of survival.

The agricultural depression can be seen to have provided two elements in the train of events which was to bring about the Development Commission. The most obvious was the strong feeling that something must be done and that the 'something' was, in substantial part at least, the responsibility of the state. In this, of course, agriculture was in no way alone, since other areas of the economy were also suffering and there were equally demands, not least from some industrialists, that the state should involve itself with some form of national planning.

The second element was perhaps less direct, but no less significant. This was the enthusiasm for innovation: new ways of working and for 'experiment' and a 'scientific' approach both to productive processes and to management. Comparisons with other European countries, especially Germany, where national development and also social welfare provision were more advanced, were made by some reformers. In many ways, too, this attitude was a continuation of the Victorian enthusiasm for science and modernisation but these attitudes had arguably not infiltrated the rural sphere, where long-established social structures too often matched equally antiquated husbandry methods.

The origins of the Development Commission do not, of course, lie exclusively within the agricultural depression. It is important to stand back from a strictly rural perspective and to see its creation as part of a broader movement towards economic and social reform. At the head of these wider issues was the concern over unemployment. Some economists had argued in the 1890s that the state should tackle unemployment by instituting systems of public works. In 1895 the Independent Labour Party promoted a programme which required public control of industry, increased education and, significantly, the state development of vacant agricultural land. Demands for a greater involvement in economic development by the state came also from the business community. Here the preferred focus was not on state ownership of the means of production but rather the creation of the necessary climate for private enterprise. Scientific research and the provision of technical education were seen as two important contributions in this direction. A third suggestion from the business quarter was for greater public investment in communications and transport infrastructure. As will be appreciated later, all three elements were to be reflected in the legislation which created the Development Commission.

These areas of education, public works, scientific research and communications were themselves to be the focus of major enquiries, instituted by the Liberal government which came to power at the end of 1905. A Departmental Committee on Agricultural Education in England and Wales reported in 1908, recommending public subsidy of experimental farming and forestry. A Consultative Committee of the Board of Education argued the following year that technical education was the key to economic growth and to unemployment relief. Also in 1909, two further reports appeared. The Royal Commission on the Canals and Inland Navigations of the United Kingdom, under the chairmanship of Lord Shuttleworth, proposed the nationalisation and development of the canal system. And finally the Royal Commission on Coast Erosion and Afforestation reported in 1909, recommending schemes of state forestry development as a particular answer to the problems of unemployment and rural population loss. All these proposals, coming from prestigious and government-inspired sources, created a demand which the Development Commission would, in part, be designed to meet.

1909 also saw the publication of the Report of the Royal Commission on the Poor Laws which had been set up in 1905 by the Conservative government. Over the period of its deliberations, the Royal Commission had encouraged a national debate about the nature of poverty, social welfare and of the role of government in policy. While there were disagreements amongst the members of the Commission, particularly as to approaches to unemployment relief, both the Majority and Minority Reports which appeared in 1909 emphasised the role of central, as opposed to local, government in

Old tins to mend – c.1908

economic and welfare policy. These views were consonant with a developing ethos, reflected in the other Reports already referred to, which stressed the need for collective and centrally-directed state policies of development and social welfare.

In one particular respect, the Royal Commission on the Poor Laws was to have an important impact upon the early working of the Development Commission. Beatrice Webb was a member of the Royal Commission but she disagreed strongly with the views of the majority of members regarding the relationship between unemployment and public works. In the Minority Report of the Commission she argued against the use of public works (and afforestation and land reclamation were seen as prime areas for such activity) simply as unemployment relief. Such 'public enterprises' should be carried out for their intrinsic national importance and not as efforts to reduce the dole queue. Her husband, Sidney, was to be appointed as a Development Commissioner in the following year. As will be seen later, the Commission was frequently to reject schemes which simply seemed disguised unemployment relief.

This chapter has outlined in brief some of the circumstances which led up to Lloyd George's Budget Statement and to the creation of the Development Commission. These circumstances led also, of course, to a much wider programme of social reform, which was to leave its mark on the country for many decades. As such, the Development Commission was but one element in a panoply of radical measures. However, the proposals to create the Commission directly addressed the growing demands for 'national development' and, from the start, focused upon the rural areas. As the next chapter will show, Lloyd George's ideas commanded substantial support across a wide political spectrum. Such support was to continue well beyond the Commission's creation and early years.

CHAPTER 2

Creating the Commission 1909-1910

By 1909 there was a substantial body of opinion existing within both the Liberal Party and the government which was in favour of some scheme for 'national development'. The focus of such development was clearly on what were viewed as 'state' industries such as forestry, land reclamation and road building. Indeed such schemes were also widely supported in the country, notably by the Labour Party which saw them as an integral part of a broader scheme of radical social and economic reform.

The 1909 Budget

It fell to Lloyd George, as Chancellor of the Exchequer, to announce the creation of a 'development fund' as part of what became known as the People's Budget of 1909. The Budget Statement was given over a period of four and a half hours on 29 April 1909. By all accounts, Lloyd George's reputation as an orator was hardly earned that afternoon. While he declared his Statement to be a 'war' budget (war, that is, against the evils of unemployment and the misuse of valuable national resources), he laboriously read his speech and his delivery was ponderous and hesitant – hardly a fitting announcement for what were to be important developments in national policy.

The Budget Statement makes it clear that considerable thought had already been given as to the areas which might benefit from the expenditure of state funds. Two major platforms of the proposed reforms were focused directly on unemployment: the creation of a system of voluntary labour exchanges and the institution of a scheme of unemployment insurance. Contrasting Britain with other countries, notably Germany, the Chancellor also announced the intention to create two new state bodies. One was to be a road board, charged with controlling the development of motor traffic and with building roads. He noted that Britain had perhaps three or four times as many motor vehicles as France and Germany and he looked forward, with some prescience perhaps, to car manufacture having a 'great future'. A problem lay, however, in the fact that this burgeoning industry was not matched by the country's road network and was evidently beginning to destroy what was there. While in the previous century, the railways had been seen as a key agent of national economic growth, the motor car looked set to take over this role in the twentieth century. For this to happen, and to prevent 'the damage done, if not to agriculture, at least to the amenities of rural life by the dust clouds which follow in the wake of these vehicles', a system of roads controlled nationally, and not by a multitude of local authorities, was needed. The cost would, he explained, be funded by the motorist.

The second creation was to be a 'development scheme'. He spoke of:

'... the millions of acres in this country which are more stripped and sterile than they were, and providing a living for fewer people than they did even a thousand years ago - acres which abroad would either be clad in profitable trees or be brought even to a higher state of cultivation ... There is much to be done for the re-settlement of neglected and forgotten areas in Britain'.

(*HANSARD*, 29 APRIL 1909, CO1.490)

The prime tools for this development were to be experiment and education, both substantially funded by the state, and focused especially on the two areas of afforestation and the encouragement of agriculture:

'The State can help by instruction, by organisation, by direction, and even, in certain cases which are outside the legitimate sphere of individual enterprise, by incurring direct responsibility ... It will include such objects as the institution of schools of forestry, the purchase and preparation of land for afforestation, the setting up of a number of experimental forests on a large scale, expenditure upon scientific research in the interests of agriculture, experimental farms, the improvement of stock ... the equipment of agencies for disseminating agricultural instruction, the encouragement and promotion of co-operation, the improvement of rural transport so as to make markets more accessible'.

(*HANSARD*, 29 APRIL 1909, CO1S.493-4)

This ambitious prospectus was to be funded partly with new money and partly from existing sources. Central government could already give grants, for example, for technical instruction, agricultural research and for harbour construction. To these would be added in the first year the sum of £200,000 to form a Development Fund, which would be administered by a body of Commissioners. Their responsibility, it was to become clear, was to advise on the spending of the Fund in response to applications for schemes which would come forward from government departments, local authorities and other non–profit-making organisations.

The support for the Chancellor's proposals, while not unanimous, was evidently substantial. In Cabinet, he had been opposed by some ministers (notably John Burns of the Local Government Board, who feared the invasion of their jurisdiction by another body) but he was powerfully supported by Asquith and Churchill. Such opposition continued into the summer of 1909 with Edwin Montagu, the Prime Minister's parliamentary private secretary, issuing a memorandum to the Prime Minister in which he suggested that these developmental activities should be vested, not in a new body, but in the existing Board of Agriculture. The reputation and status of the Board would thereby be enhanced in a way which he felt was warranted by the political importance of agriculture. Lloyd George did not intend to create a new executive body, as a memorandum in July 1909 from his private secretary, Ralph Hartrey, made clear, but the concerns were understandable. As will be seen, such territorial jealousy would continue for years.

Paradoxically, the reality, that the Commissioners' functions really were only advisory and not executive, would equally recur over the subsequent years as a continuing limitation to the power of the Commission until the 1980s.

Opposition and criticism in the House of Commons to the proposals in the Budget Statement was relatively limited. Indeed at various times during his speech the Chancellor received applause from the other side of the House. Both Liberal and Labour members broadly supported the proposals, and the focus upon aiding the countryside would have appealed to many Conservatives. There was some dissent: some members, for example Austen Chamberlain, objecting to the raiding of existing funds to supply the new scheme, while others expressed surprise that so great an agenda of action was to be funded from so relatively small a sum of money.

Vocal opposition was, however, forthcoming, notably from the die-hard Conservative Sir Frederick Banbury. He, too, expressed surprise at the modest level of new money to be given to the Development Fund in its first year, but he suspected that the Chancellor, once his main purpose was achieved, would soon be asking for more. In the main, however, he objected to the breadth of the proposals contained in a Budget speech:

> 'It is five or six King's Speeches rolled into one …We listened to every Radical fad which we
> have ever heard communicated but which had nothing whatever to do with the Budget
> Question. When the right hon. Gentleman told us that he was going to start model farms,
> afforestation, colleges for agriculture, colleges for technical something or other, places for
> improving the breed of cattle, and all sorts of other things, I watched my hon. Friend beside
> me endeavouring to put them down on paper; but when he got down nine or ten he gave it
> up, and so did I.'
>
> (HANSARD, 29 APRIL 1909, CO1.583)

The Development and Road Improvement Funds Bill

Sir Frederick returned to the attack when the Chancellor of the Exchequer introduced the necessary Bill to enact the Development Commission to the House on 26 August 1909. He and other Conservatives objected on a number of technical grounds. Lloyd George had outlined the objectives of the Bill in the Westminster Gazette before he had given it to the members of the House. Moreover, they argued, there was a further fault in that the name of the Bill was not on the order paper. Above all, they complained that the Bill was, in effect, a 'money' bill and as such should not be considered in the normal way since no 'money resolution' had been introduced. These objections were overruled by the Deputy Speaker and the Bill moved to its Second Reading, where the main debate took place. Originally planned for 30 August, that day was, in the event, given over to a consideration of the *Housing, Town Planning etc. Bill*, and the Second Reading therefore took place on 6 September 1909.

The debate was opened by the Chancellor who was followed by Lord Robert Cecil, the member for Marylebone. He attacked both the development and the road proposals, seeing in them 'all the traces of megalomania'. Such a view was perhaps encouraged when, later on in the debate, Lloyd George's proposal was effusively welcomed by the Labour leader Keir Hardie as the 'most revolutionary measure' that had been introduced by a British government. It was thus hardly surprising to hear Lord Robert Cecil argue that the proposals were 'part of the Socialist programme', as he tried to convince the House of the enormity of the proposals. Members should not be fooled into thinking that the Chancellor was putting forward a modest scheme:

'... so far from this being for small instructional matters in agriculture and forestry, it really extends to the whole field of industrial and commercial activity'.

(*HANSARD*, 6 SEPTEMBER 1909, COL.910)

Cecil's attack on the Development Fund encapsulated several objections, which a minority of members shared. Above all, they saw the proposal as an unprecedented incursion of the state into economic affairs which were properly the concern of business. Secondly, they resisted what they saw as the creation of yet another government body. Thirdly, they were mightily suspicious of the likely future cost of the schemes, believing that the relatively modest initial allocation was but the precursor of greater raids on the public purse. Finally, they saw in the advisory role of the new Commissioners a real prospect of favouritism and corruption in the granting of money from the Fund.

However, this opposition was numerically small. At the first division just twenty-five voted against the motion. Following a failed attempt to get the Bill referred to a committee of the whole House, and an amendment by Sir Frederick Banbury to limit the Fund to just £100,000, Lloyd George finally put the motion at 1.55am on the morning of 7 September. A somewhat depleted House, hardly surprising in view of the hour, voted 103 in favour with just six Conservative votes against.

While the arguments of the Bill's opposers, which were outlined above, clearly carried little weight with other Members, they were later to be important in that they explain many of the aspects of the way in which the Development Commission was to work in the future. On the positive side, the concerns as to the 'revolutionary' role which the Commission might play were to some extent justified. As subsequent chapters will tell, the activities of the Commission ranged widely and it was responsible for a great deal of innovation.

But there was a negative side as well and it can be argued that, in an attempt to counter the criticisms, Lloyd George effectively hobbled his new creation from the very outset. In the short term, the worry about corruption led him to take many weeks to appoint the new Commissioners, such was the concern about probity. In the longer term, as the next chapter will show, the Commissioners seem to have been so aware of their responsibilities in advising on how the Development Fund should be spent that they consistently underspent, and arguably thereby were too cautious in supporting new schemes of development. Above all, however, the assurance from the Chancellor that he was not creating a new executive agency but merely an advisory body proved correct. The Commission would for long be beholden to the Treasury to agree its proposals and as such would lack the freedom of action for which its creator had hoped.

The Development Act and the appointment of Commissioners

The *Development and Road Improvement Funds Act* (9 Ed. 7c 47) was finally passed on 3 December 1909, under which a development fund was to be created and advice given to the Treasury by five Commissioners as to how it should be spent. The range of its activities included agriculture and rural industries, forestry, land drainage and reclamation, rural transport, harbour construction and improvement of harbours and inland navigation, and the improvement of fisheries. A final purpose allowed for the support of 'any other purpose calculated to promote the economic development of the United Kingdom'.

Lloyd George's attention then turned to the question of the appointment of Commissioners. In the short term, however, there was a General Election to fight. Asquith and the Liberals were returned to power in January 1910, though with a narrow majority. The Chancellor had, however, been giving thought to possible names for appointment to the Commission. He was consistently lobbied, especially from the agricultural community, and he was inundated with letters from individuals putting themselves forward or suggesting their colleagues. It is interesting to note that, of all such letters now kept in the Public Record Office, not one related to anyone eventually appointed.

Lloyd George fully recognised that, in the appointment of the Commissioners, he had to balance many interests. First, political geography had to be satisfied, with Scotland, Wales and Ireland duly represented. Then the farming lobby had to be recognised, as had the forestry interest. He probably realised that this balancing act would be difficult, if not impossible, with just five Commissioners and so made plans to increase that number. In the meantime he proceeded to take advice and, unknown to the individuals concerned, considered the possibility of suitable candidates. He was frequently asked in the House as to when he would announce the appointments. His response, as to Lord Balcarres in March, was that it was 'a rather difficult matter' and that he was 'taking my time over it'.

An increase in the number of Commissioners would require an amendment to the original Act and so on 27 April 1910 Lloyd George introduced the proposal to increase the number to ten. The day before he had telegraphed several prospective Commissioners to enlist them with the injunction 'important Chancellor should receive answer if possible tomorrow'. In fact he left approaching one future Commissioner (Sidney Webb) as late as four o'clock on the afternoon of 28 April.

The reason for this request for a prompt response became clear in the House the next day. In some contrast to the Budget Speech of the previous year, Lloyd George was at his parliamentary best. He proposed an increase to ten Commissioners. The opposition (Sir Frederick Banbury again) argued that this was too many and, moreover, objected that it was wrong to amend something which as yet had not operated. Lloyd George countered, after eventually naming some of the proposed appointees, with an amended proposal for just eight Commissioners. The opposition conceded the point, and the Chancellor then announced the remaining names to represent the Irish and the Welsh interests. He had simply got what he wanted all along.

Eight Development Commissioners

The Royal Warrant appointing the Commissioners and setting the order of their retirement, was not signed until some two weeks later (12 May 1910) and then not by King Edward VII, who had died on 6 May, but by his successor George V. The warrant was countersigned by Winston Churchill, who had been made Home Secretary in February following the election. Provision had been made in the Act for two of the Commissioners, including the Chairman, to be paid and a sum had been allocated for this purpose.

The eight Commissioners who were appointed were:

- **Lord Richard Cavendish**, a former Liberal Unionist MP and the nephew of the Duke of Devonshire. Cavendish was appointed as Chairman, a post he was to retain until his death in 1946. His appointment was clearly seen as an uncontroversial one in a situation where factions and interests were bound to arise.

- **Sir Francis Hopwood**, an eminent civil servant who was Permanent Under-Secretary of State for the Colonies. He was appointed as Vice-Chairman and, together with Cavendish, was to be a paid Commissioner.

- **Saint-Hill Eardley-Wilmot**, who had been Inspector-General of Forests to the government of India, and accordingly was seen to provide the necessary expertise in forestry.

- **Henry Jones Davies**, the County Land Agent for Carmarthenshire.

- **Michael Andrew Ennis**, a member of the Congested Districts Board in Ireland.

- **William Stowell Haldane**, a solicitor and the Crown Agent for Scotland.

- **Alfred Daniel Hall**, the Director of the Rothamsted Experimental Station.

- **Sidney James Webb**, the social reformer and Fabian.

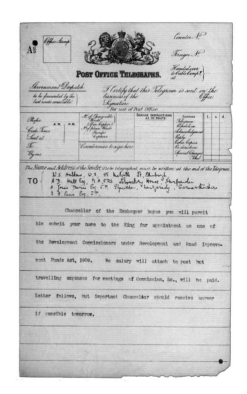

The telegraph sent by Lloyd George to prospective Commissioners on 26 April 1910

It was these eight men who met on 25 May 1910 at the first statutory meeting of the new Development Commission.

CHAPTER 3

Rusticus expectans:
early activity 1918-1920

The public reception given to the new Development Commission was decidedly mixed. *The Times* had reported the appointment of the Commissioners on 28 April and that had prompted 'a correspondent' to comment with invective two days later. He criticised the long delay in making the appointments, which he believed had been increased in number 'for no good reason', and went on to comment:

> 'Seldom has so small a sum, of such uncertain source, been more effusively bruited or stirred so many hopes in so many societies'.

The delays, he felt, had simply given time for 'the beggars' to mobilise their importuning:

> 'At their first meeting the Commissioners will find that they have to sift an extraordinary farrago of claims ... if the Commissioners pay heed to a tithe of the claims, the sum at their disposal will be dissipated in doles which will please many people without essentially benefiting any'.

If this was a widely held view then one of its comments at least was correct. The Act and the proposed Commission were especially welcomed by the farming fraternity. At a meeting of the Farmers' Club on 31 January 1910, the Secretary, H. Trustram Eve, read a paper outlining the principles of the Act. His view was that: 'no more important Act has been passed affecting the welfare of agriculture'; that there would be 'a competition and scramble for the money'; and, despite apparent promises by the Chancellor of the Exchequer that £250,000 should be earmarked for agriculture, 'it is quite certain that unless the agricultural organisations use their influence, many other interests will obtain more than their fair share of the money and agriculture will be left in the cold'. The Irish faction was seen as a particularly greedy 'beggar' ('There is nothing Ireland does not ask for but what she gets'), and grave doubts were also expressed as to the competence of the County Councils as potential recipients of the Fund.

In the audience that day was Daniel Hall, then Director of the Lawes Experimental Station at Rothamsted in Hertfordshire. Although he did not know it at the time, three months later he was to be appointed as a Commissioner and so

Daniel Hall, 1912

his contribution to the meeting gives an interesting light on the early direction which the Commission's work took. Hall, who as will be seen was to be very influential in this work, declared in the discussion which followed the paper that his personal attitude towards the new venture was that of the *rusticus expectans*. It is clear that, while they might not use the Latin tag in so scholarly a fashion, the mass of farmers concurred in this view. Hall went on to emphasise the importance of agricultural research, welcoming the Act as the first time that the state had accepted responsibility for this activity, and even highlighting the potential as he saw it of crops such as sugar beet and tobacco. He rather played down the need for substantial investment in education, a somewhat curious comment, perhaps, from someone who had been the first Principal of Wye College and who was shortly to draft out a key memorandum on education for the new Commission.

Agreeing procedures

The first business meeting of the new Commission was held in temporary accommodation in the Board Room at the Treasury on 1 July 1910. The Commission was to move to more permanent quarters in Queen Anne's Chambers, Westminster, in the following January. The minutes of the first twenty-eight meetings until late 1912 (and indeed those of the eighty-second to eighty-fourth meetings) are now missing, but it is clear from the First Report of the Development Commissioners that they were much concerned with understanding their new powers (and their limitations) and in agreeing procedures. If an application to the Development Fund came from a government department, then it was directed straight to the Commission. If it came from an outside body, such as a county council or a non-profit making organisation, the application was sent first to the relevant government department for comment. In any event, all recommendations for grants from the Commission had to be routed back to the Treasury for final approval. This cumbersome procedure, necessitated by the terms of the Act, was to handicap the Commission for many years. It possessed no power of its own to grant money and had no executive ability to undertake work itself. This, coupled with the ponderous involvement of the Treasury and other government departments, inevitably limited the activity of the Commission. It also meant that credit for any successes or innovations tended to accrue not to the Commission, but of the agency actually doing the work, thus limiting the Commission's ability to achieve a high profile. Moreover it resulted in very significant underspending from the Fund for many years. Despite these undoubted problems, it is clear that in certain key areas the Commission accomplished a great deal in these early years.

The Commissioners were also concerned to define the limits of such power as they had under the Act of 1910. Certain matters were very clear, particularly the inability to grant to profit-making bodies. As the First Report stated: 'The Fund shall not go into the pockets of private individuals'. Another definitional concern related to the terms of reference. Just what was 'any other purpose calculated to promote the economic development of the United Kingdom'? Somewhat pedantically they took advice and were told that 'those words must be read in the light of the preceding words of the sub-section, and cannot therefore be held to cover all economic development, but only purposes cognate to and *in eodem genere* with those expressly named'. In the early years of operation this advice probably did stop the Commissioners from being as innovative and as interventionist as they might have been.

Some further principles were also established in this first year of operation. No money could be used to supplant existing government expenditure or local rates. However, Commissioners would look favourably on schemes where grants from the Fund would call forth expenditure from other sources – an early example of matching funding. Further, any loans made from the Fund were expected to be 'directly remunerative sooner or later' and hence 'the Commissioners see no reason why the Fund should provide money and not obtain at least repayment and reasonable interest if the anticipation of the promoters are fulfilled'.

Setting an agenda

The first meetings of the Commission were inevitably much occupied with responding to applications to the Development Fund. In the period to March 1911 some 170 requests were made to the Treasury from non-governmental bodies, with a further twenty-four coming directly to the Commission from government departments. But, to their credit, the Commissioners agreed from the start that they should respond to applications in the light of a declared strategy and not on an *ad hoc* basis. In this way a comprehensive set of policies would be developed whereby a defined direction would be made clear and duplication avoided.

This principle was enunciated in the First Report and the example of agricultural research given to illustrate the point. On this basis it is fair to argue that the hand of Daniel Hall can be clearly seen in this important proposal. As will be seen, Hall was directly responsible for the outlining of such a strategy for agricultural research, a development which was to have a major influence upon the operation of this aspect of British science until the present day.

Hall was also probably behind the setting of another important principle – that dispositions from the Fund should go to schemes which were seen as innovative (and which might not otherwise happen) and that two key elements should be experiment and demonstration. The approach was natural to the one trained scientist on the Commission and it was also supported by Sidney Webb, who saw it in much the same way as Hall from his perspective of social enquiry.

Before leaving the matter of general principles, another point must be made. Even a cursory reading of Reports and Minutes from these early days gives the reader an immediate impression of the seriousness of approach which the Commissioners took. No topic or application was considered lightly. Commissioners met very regularly indeed and even in wartime there would be five or six meetings a year. A meeting called on 7 August 1914, just four years since the first meeting, was the fifty-second occasion on which Commissioners had met. Moreover, these were not the only meetings, since sub-committees were set up early on to consider particular topics, such as forestry and fisheries. Lloyd George had been aware of the need for probity, care and an absence of corruption in the membership of his new Commission. His choices amply rewarded him to the point, some might argue, of a pedantic concern for detail and a positively high, even narrow, minded approach to public expenditure.

Personalities

Before consideration is given to the developing programme of work undertaken by the Commission in this early period, comment should be made about some of the personalities involved. Such was the care taken by Commissioners that policy directions were often the result of an individual with a particular interest. Moreover, while the officers who served the Commission, especially in the post of Secretary, were clearly as committed and assiduous as the members, they frequently appear as somewhat shadowy figures, content to advise and to carry out the decisions which were taken by Commissioners. The evidence of the early meetings strongly suggest that it was, quite properly, the Commissioners themselves who were investigating applications in some depth and were then making their own decisions.

Lord Richard Cavendish, who served as Chairman until his death in 1946, had been chosen as an acceptable candidate to all parties. Little of his personality comes through from a reading of Reports or papers, though it may be assumed that the attention to detail which characterised the working of the Commission came, in part at least, from his leadership. The first Secretary to the Commission, H.E. Dale, said of him: 'by character as by inherited position he was fortified against all attempts … to turn him from what he thought right … he possessed a full measure of the slow solid common-sense which for generations has distinguished the great house of Cavendish'.

Sir Francis Hopwood, the paid Vice-Chairman, effectively played little part in the workings of the Commission. He had been highly reluctant to leave his successful career in the Colonial Office for what he obviously felt would be the backwater of the Development Commission. In practice, he was absent in India for much of the time and resigned within a year of his appointment to return briefly to the Colonial Office before becoming a member of the Privy Council and a civil Lord of the Admiralty under Winston Churchill in 1912.

Lord Richard Cavendish with King George V at the British Industries Fair, 1926

Haldane, Ennis and Jones-Davies all had agricultural interests together with other public appointments. Their role was intended to balance any suspected English bias in the other five members and they inevitably took a particular interest in applications coming respectively from Scotland, Ireland and Wales.

That left three Commissioners, all of them viewed as 'specialists' in their particular fields. Especially notable was the great social reformer, Sidney Webb. He brought to the Commission a wealth of experience in the fields of education, local government and of social conditions in

England generally. As mentioned earlier, a particular link with the origins of the Development Commission lay in the fact that his wife Beatrice had been a member of the Royal Commission on the Poor Laws from 1906 to 1909. His commitment, not so much to the direct 'development' of natural resources, but rather to the principles of social and economic improvement, of state involvement and responsibility, and of the commitment to co-operation which was explicit in the Act, was undoubted. Not for nothing did he and his wife have within their wedding rings inscribed the motto *pro bono publico*.

Saint-Hill Eardley-Wilmot provided the forestry expertise within the Commission. He had recently retired from being Inspector-General of Forests in India. He was to remain a Development Commissioner only until May 1913 when he retired, as had been determined in the Royal Warrant of 1910, though he continued as Forestry Advisor to the Commission.

The final expert, and the member of the Commission who was to make the most significant contribution to its work during its formative years, was Alfred Daniel Hall. Hall was, by 1910, a much-respected agricultural scientist. He had been the first Principal of the South-Eastern Agricultural College at Wye in Kent from which, as mentioned earlier, he had moved in 1902 to become the Director of the Lawes Agricultural Experimental Station at Rothamsted. Hall's appointment to the Commission was important in several respects. First, he brought to its meetings a deep knowledge of science coupled with a logical mind and singular ability to lay out a strategic programme of work. Second, he was from 1912 (until his departure to become Secretary to the Board of Agriculture in 1917) to be appointed as a full-time Commissioner, paid from money which had been freed up by the departure of Sir Francis Hopwood. The early commitment of the Commissioners to a strategic, as opposed to an *ad hoc*, approach to applications from the Development Fund, and the character of that strategic approach were very substantially due to Hall's work. The contribution he made to the work of the Development Commission is especially clear from the account given by H.E. Dale in his biography of Daniel Hall.

Two further personalities, both of whom made a very important contribution to the Commission's work, should be noted at this point. The departure of Hopwood in 1912 was followed a year later by the appointment of Vaughan Nash. He had been one of Asquith's private secretaries and was to serve the Commission until 1929. Nash became Vice-Chairman and proved himself from the outset to be an enthusiastic and committed member, especially later in matters relating to rural industry and social and community development in rural areas.

The other influential character was Thomas (later Sir Thomas) Middleton. He had come from a Scottish farming background and initially trained as an engineer. Following a successful academic career at Aberystwyth and Newcastle, he had become Drapers Professor of Agriculture at Cambridge in 1902 before leaving to be Assistant Secretary in the Intelligence Division of the Board of Agriculture in 1906. Middleton was eventually to become a Development Commissioner in 1919 but his significance at this early stage lies in his co-operation with Daniel Hall. The effective co-operation between the Board of Agriculture and the Development Commission was to prove a very powerful engine for agricultural development. The two men each brought something different to the partnership: Hall as the intellectual and the scientist and Middleton as the consummate administrator and committed government servant. In other ways they shared qualities. Dale, in his biography of Hall, is positively sycophantic in his praise, but there was clearly some truth in the assertion that:

> 'He [Middleton] had much in common with Hall, untiring industry supported on robust health, thoroughness, tenacity, absolute honesty in word and deed, and true geniality springing from a profound kindness of heart; respect, confidence and affection followed them wherever they went'.

The developing programme of work

Although, as was noted earlier, the first meetings of the Development Commission were often concerned with matters of principle and procedure, the Commission had to get to grips at an early stage with a large number of applications to the Development Fund. *The Times* correspondent who had warned of 'an extraordinary farrago of claims' had perhaps exaggerated, but judged by quantity alone he had been right.

The need for speed in responding to applications and the assiduousness of Commissioners in meeting (no fewer than thirty meetings by the middle of December 1912) meant that the broad programme of future work was settled very early on. The table of contents (Fig. 3.1) taken from the Third Report ending 31 March 1913 gives a clear indication of both the content and relative importance given to particular topics. This pattern had been established from the very outset and was to be the broad structure of operations up until the outbreak of the Second World War.

Agricultural research and education

The dominance given to various aspects of agriculture is plain – Trustram Eve's exhortation to the members of the Farmers' Club had obviously not fallen upon deaf ears. But, beyond the obvious fact that the Act of 1910 had concentrated much upon agriculture, it is fair to argue that this dominance was also due in large part to that synergetic duo, Hall and Middleton.

In December 1910, barely six months into the Commission's work, members received two memoranda, one on agricultural research and the other on agricultural education. Both were written by Daniel Hall – indeed the typescripts of both memoranda have 'Mr Hall's' written in before the title, seemingly by the Secretary.

Hall's *Memorandum on Agricultural Research* set out in just eighteen foolscap pages the outline of a system of research centres which was to last for decades. Indeed, the pattern he put forward is still discernible today. He recognised three types of research. 'Research proper' involved acquiring new knowledge 'though its practical outcome may appear remote'. Then there were investigations into particular subjects 'which propose a definite and immediate practical end'. Finally he noted the need for demonstrations of the application of known principles. His proposals concentrated on the first two categories since, he argued, they called 'for institutions dealing continuously and systematically with the subject rather than for grants allocated to specific investigations'.

Thus Hall argued for a principle of scientific research which was not to be circumscribed by narrow concepts of a customer: contractor principle and narrow attitudes of financial accounting. Indeed in the *Memorandum* he stated: 'I should be very sorry to have to justify on a monetary basis much of the work going on at Rothamsted'. He then went on to list the existing seventeen centres which carried out research of this type. These were:

1. Rothamsted Experimental Station.
2. The Department of Agriculture, University of Cambridge.
3. The Animal Institute, Department of Agriculture, University of Cambridge.
4. South-Eastern Agricultural College, Wye, Kent.
5. Midland Dairy and Agricultural College, Kingston, Nottinghamshire.
6. University of Leeds.
7. Armstrong College, Newcastle-upon-Tyne.
8. North of Scotland Agricultural College, Aberdeen.
9. West of Scotland Agricultural College.
10. The Royal Agricultural Society experimental farm at Woburn, Bedfordshire.
11. The Experimental Fruit Farm, Ridgmount.
12. The John Innes Institute, Merton, Surrey.
13. The Fruit and Cider Institute, Long Ashton, Bristol.
14. The Royal Horticultural Society, Wisley, Surrey.
15. The Research Association, Aberdeen.
16. The Irish Department of Agriculture.
17. The Royal Veterinary College, London.

Finally, he outlined the main research areas which he believed should be concentrated in one, or at most two, centres, together with his tentative suggestions, where research currently existed, as to where these centres might be:

1. *Plant nutrition.* Rothamsted.
2. *Plant physiology and pathology.*
3. *Plant diseases (fungal and insects).* A southern (Wye) and a northern (Edinburgh) centre were suggested.
4. *Plant breeding.* Cambridge and/or the John Innes Institute.
5. *Animal breeding.* Cambridge and possibly also a centre in Ireland.
6. *Veterinary and pathological research.*
7. *Dairy work.* Possibly two institutes, one dealing with milk production (Kilmarnock or Glasgow); the other dealing with bacterial and fungal infections of cheese, possibly at the Midland Dairy Institute.
8. *Fruit and cider.* Long Ashton.
9. *Forestry.* Aberdeen or possibly Cambridge.

Fig. 3.1 The early pattern of work, taken from the Third Report of the Development Commissioners, 1912-1913

DEVELOPMENT COMMISSION:

CONTENTS.

Some of these suggestions were carried through in practice, while the list of specialisms and of centres was modified and added to in the next few years. However, whatever the research area, Hall was adamant that certain key principles should guide the work. All research was to be properly costed and accounted for; each centre was to concentrate on its particular specialism and was to publicise the results of the research widely and in annual reports. Finally, the Board of Agriculture, through which government department the necessary money from the Development Fund would be routed, could call freely for advice upon the expertise in the institutes. The *Memorandum* is understandably Daniel Hall's personal agenda – he had been thinking along these lines for years and at last had his opportunity to effect his dreams. Moreover his preferences can be seen in his listings: Rothamsted, of which he was Director, was viewed with justification as the prime centre; Wye, where he had been Principal in the 1890s; Cambridge, where his friend Thomas Middleton had been Professor of Agriculture.

With the *Memorandum* to give strategic guidance, and with scientists and others becoming aware of the new Development Commission's likely preferences as to where grants might be expected, there began an unprecedented period in which research was funded and new research institutes were created. In the first year of operation, the Commission granted the sum of £13,656 towards the research being carried out in the institutes and universities, together with a further £3,000 towards research elsewhere. In the period from 1911 (when the Research Institute in Plant Physiology was created at Imperial College, London University) to 1928 (with the foundation of the Hannah Dairy Research Institute at Auchincruve, Ayrshire), no fewer than eleven research centres were created, eight of them in the short period from 1911 to the outbreak of war.

The topics which Hall had outlined for priority were followed up, sometimes at the centres where he had noted current work. A national centre for research in dairying was based at Reading in 1912, linked to the University College. In the same year the Plant Breeding Institute was created at Cambridge, as was the Rowett Research Institute for animal nutrition in Aberdeen. A research centre for horticulture at East Malling in Kent followed in 1913, linked to the college at Wye. In an interesting and far-sighted departure from the 1910 list, the Commission provided funds in 1913 to create the Agricultural Economics Research Institute at the University of Oxford. Its first Director, until he retired in 1945, was Charles Stuart Orwin, one of the first thirteen students whom Hall had welcomed to the newly-founded South-Eastern Agricultural College at Wye in November 1894.

Hall's *Memorandum on agricultural education* was much less prescriptive than that on agricultural research. In part this was because there was significantly more activity already going on in this area, especially under the jurisdiction of the county councils which had, in a number of cases, opened up colleges of agriculture using funds originating from alcohol taxation ('whisky money') in the 1890s. More recently there had been a major review of agricultural education under the chairmanship of Lord Reay, which had reported in 1908 and to which Hall (and Middleton) had contributed. Having said that, while there were ideas as to how things might develop, the funds were often lacking.

While some important issues of principle needed to be settled first (for example, to what extent should agricultural education be developed away from the rather uninspiring control of the county councils), Commissioners followed Hall's advice and committed themselves at an early stage to funding agricultural education broadly along the lines that had been suggested by the Reay Committee. Thus farm institutes were to be founded in each county and the sum of £80,000 was set aside for this task in the first year, with the intention of agreeing a further £325,000 for the period up to March 1916. By the outbreak of war in 1914 six had been set up and others were to follow, though complete coverage was never achieved. Linked to these institutes there was to be a county agricultural adviser who would provide the link with the farming community. From 1912, a grant of £12,000 per year was awarded from the Development Fund for this purpose.

In addition to funding the new creations, the Commissioners also considered applications from existing institutions. Thus, at their twenty-ninth meeting they agreed a grant of £6,000 to go to Armstrong College, Newcastle, and also agreed funding for the North of Scotland College of Agriculture. Further, they offered £9,000 towards the estimated total cost of £30,000 needed to create the Seale Hayne College of Agriculture near Newton Abbot in Devon. At the next meeting, in December 1912, they were faced with an application for an increase in the building grant to £6,000 from Hall's old college at Wye. Following a report from Middleton at the Board of Agriculture, which was distinctly critical of both the administration of the college and its financial position, the Commissioners left the matter to be decided by the Chairman, Vice-Chairman and Hall himself.

Experimentation and co-operation in agriculture

Beyond the schemes for research and education, the new Commission stuck to the brief which had been outlined in the Act. Experimentation with new crops was a component of this and grants were made to investigate the cultivation of sugar beet in Norfolk and also of tobacco and of hemp for flax production. The activities involving tobacco were less than successful, though a Tobacco Growing Association had been formed, but hemp growing was to receive a boost during the war when flax was needed in the production of aircraft fuselages. After initial losses on the experimental farm at Cantley in Norfolk, the cultivation of sugar beet became an undoubted success.

A final element within the strategy for agriculture, and again one enjoined in the Act of 1910, was the encouragement of co-operation. The models of success in this area which were before the Commission were Denmark and Ireland – but it would become clear that the English farmer was not of a co-operative bent. For a few years the Commission saw some success for its financial efforts in Ireland, where it supported the Irish Agricultural Organisation Society, founded in 1894 by the great apostle of agricultural co-operation, Sir Horace Plunkett. Funding of the Agricultural Organisation Society in England, starting with £3,000 in the first year to allow the appointment of a general secretary, office staff and 'competent organisers', was to prove far less successful.

Forestry

If agriculture proved in the early stages to have the lion's share of the Commissioners' attention, other matters were also of concern. Forestry was prime amongst these and the Act had made possible a potentially ambitious programme involving the creation of 'schools of forestry', the acquisition of land for planting and the creation of experimental forests.

From the outset, two important principles guided the new Commission in its policy on forestry. The First Report makes it clear that, as in agriculture, there was an overall concern regarding the state of research and education; there was, Commissioners believed, an absolute requirement for 'effective education in forestry at suitable centres regulated by organised research'. The second principle was enunciated in the statement that 'no scheme of State afforestation on a large scale can be considered until the economics is assessed'.

These two principles lay at the heart of what, in retrospect, must be judged as a distinct failure by the Development Commission in this key area, a failure which, eventually, would result in forestry being removed from the Commission's remit on the creation of the Forestry Commission in 1919. This is not to say that Commissioners neglected the topic. In one of their earliest meetings they had received a comprehensive scheme for forestry in England and Wales from the Board of Agriculture and over several meetings debated the need for advisory work, instruction, research, demonstration plantations and the like. Special meetings of the Commission were called in February and May 1913 to discuss forestry. They also responded to the remit to encourage new afforestation by lending money from the Fund to local authorities. Thus in 1913 they loaned money to Liverpool City Corporation to purchase 4,000 acres of land around Lake Vyrnwy in Wales at £200 per acre for water-gathering grounds.

It would seem, above all, that the apparent size and cost of afforestation simply frightened the Commissioners and so they retreated from the potential of expansive action to ground on which they felt safe, predominantly education and research. By 1913 they were stressing their own limitations – 'afforestation of even 100,000 acres ... is scarcely feasible' (Third Report). As will be seen later, the Commissioners appeared obsessed about the amount of money which they were given for the Development Fund. They focused on the first five years of operation and attempted to calculate what would be needed in this (and indeed other) areas until 1916. For forestry the Commissioners said:

> 'For the period till 1916, which must necessarily be in the main a period of forestry education and research (accompanied by assistance to local authorities undertaking the afforestation of areas under their control), they think that probably £350,000 will cover all the expenditure which can profitably be incurred'.
>
> (SECOND REPORT, PERIOD ENDING MARCH 1912)

There were other factors which explain this cautious record. The focus on agriculture which has been noted probably meant that other areas suffered. Daniel Hall had some interest in forestry but he was not likely to push it forward at the expense of agricultural research and education. The appointment of Eardley-Wilmot, who was the forestry specialist, came to an end in May 1913 and, although he was nominally appointed as Forestry Advisor to the Commission until 1919, his place was not filled until the next year.

Then again, there were other agencies which were looking at forestry. Barely a year after the creation of the Commission the President of the Board of Agriculture appointed an Advisory Committee on Forestry under Sir Stafford Howard. Their brief included much that was in common with that of the Development Commission – experimentation, demonstration areas and 'the instruction of woodmen'. A further requirement was to consider a forestry survey. By July of 1912 they had issued their report, which included proposals for the survey and for a 5,000-acre experimental forest. At the same time there were stirrings in the private forestry sector. The English Forestry Association was formed in 1912 with objectives which especially focused on timber marketing. Government was also willing to encourage private forestry and, in 1913, the Board of Agriculture brought in an advisory scheme to help private owners in the management of their woodlands.

The final explanation as to why the Development Commission was effectively sidelined in the area of forestry is related to the war. At the outbreak of hostilities the United Kingdom was importing some 400 million cubic feet of timber per annum. So long as reserves remained reasonably high, there was little worry, but with the onset of the German attacks on merchant shipping from early 1915, concern grew about timber supplies. A Home-Grown Timber Committee was appointed in November 1915 (the Acland Committee) with a practical brief to organise home supplies and contribute to the war effort. These duties were effectively continued when the committee was replaced by the Directorate of Timber Supplies in March 1917.

A comment by Sir William Schlich, Professor of Forestry at Oxford, in the *Quarterly Journal of Forestry* for 1915, while not referring directly to the Development Commission, delivers a harsh verdict on public authorities' inaction:

'...very little has as yet been done to increase the area under forest. Too much talking and too little action – that is the long and short of it ... Demonstration areas and Schools of Forestry are all very well, but they will not materially increase the timber supply of the country ...

Action, and again action, is what we need rather than these ever recurring Commissions and Committees'.

Other activities

While agriculture, and to some extent forestry, provided from the outset the bulk of the Development Commission's portfolio, other areas of involvement had been envisaged. In some of these areas there appeared little activity. Thus early Reports of the Commissioners express concern that very few applications were being received regarding land reclamation and drainage. They hoped, particularly after the passing of the Land Drainage Act in 1914, that more activity would be forthcoming but felt, of course, that they were only able to respond to suggestions and applications from outside.

In the area of rural transport there was also relatively little movement, again because of a paucity of applications to the Fund. At the end of its third year of operation, the Commission could report just three applications under this heading. Two related to the much-vaunted interest in 'light railways' (which were never to be important in rural development) while the third was for a 'motor car service' from Hailsham to Boreham Street in Sussex, which was to be run on a non-profit basis (as it had to be to qualify for grant) by the Herstmonceux and District Farmers' Club. In this last can be seen an interesting foreshadowing of the interest in voluntary transport some seven decades on, which would be supported by the Commission in a much more thorough and professional way.

Much more activity was discernible in the area of fisheries' development and especially in the construction and improvement of harbours. Early grants were given (for example, to the Irish Department of Agriculture to encourage the instruction in the use of motor engines by fishermen) and significant sums either granted or loaned to harbour authorities, especially in Ireland and Scotland. The Commission felt that the creation of the Development Fund had inevitably encouraged both government departments and harbour authorities to bring forward plans which otherwise could never have been financed. Early in 1912 they estimated that, after a first flush of such applications, the numbers would fall off and that a total of £450,000 would 'easily meet the reasonable claims likely to be made on the Fund from all parts of the United Kingdom up to 1916'.

Overall, some two thirds of the Commission's expenditure went on agriculture, in carrying out the schemes which had been outlined and fostered by Daniel Hall. Roughly another twenty-five per cent went on fisheries and harbours, both areas where there were local authorities and boards with schemes in mind for public expenditure. A further five per cent was spent on forestry.

The early years – an assessment

This chapter has considered the operations of the Development Commission during its first eight years, a period coinciding with the development of a set of principles and of an agenda for the work of the Commission. It also coincides roughly, and significantly, with the period during which Daniel Hall made a major contribution to the work of the new organisation. As was noted, it was he who from a very early stage mapped out, with his ally at the Board of Agriculture, Thomas Middleton, the Commission's role in agriculture and he became doubly influential during his time as a full-time Commissioner from the spring of 1912 until his departure early in 1917 to join the Board of Agriculture under its new President, Rowland Prothero (later Lord Ernle).

It is tempting to consider just what an Audit Commission would have made of the Development Commission after its first eight years. On the credit side there was an undoubted success story to be told in the area of agricultural research and, possibly to a lesser extent, in education. An amazingly rapid start had been made in the creation of a system of agricultural research centres which was, as the century continued, to build for this country a reputation second to none. For that contribution alone it could be argued that Lloyd George's creation was a resounding success. Equally the money provided year by year to the developing pattern of institutes, colleges and university departments, though never perhaps being as complete in its coverage as Hall had hoped, created a world-class system.

Again in other areas – the development of new crops, the improvement in animal breeding and in the improvement of harbours and the development of fisheries – there were success stories and local investment, which would simply not have happened without the Development Fund.

On the debit side there were first of all the failures. Obvious examples were in the area of agricultural co-operation, at least outside of Ireland, and in some experimental schemes, such as those for the cultivation of tobacco and the development of light railways. But the main criticism which can be laid at the door of the Commission during these early years is that there were areas of their broad brief where little action took place. The case of forestry is perhaps the most obvious as was seen above. Here, and in other areas, Commissioners seemed just to discuss and not to take any action. As a result, those authorities outside the Commission either ignored it or simply viewed it as a possible source of money for their own activities. This attitude became more pronounced after the outbreak of war in late 1914, when, understandably, the focus of the nation was on matters of food and timber production. Here, arguably, was a major opportunity for the Commission to make its mark. It can hardly be said to have done so.

The Commissioners at the outset had high hopes that their work would be much needed. A special meeting was called on 7 August 1914 at which it was decided to make a public announcement of a call for grants and 'to make immediately available the whole of the funds so unallocated, amounting to nearly a million pounds' (Minutes of fifty-second meeting). This call seems to have been largely ineffective. The Commission appeared surprised that their potential remained so unrecognised. As a postscript to the Fourth Report of the Development Commission, presumably added late in 1914, they referred to the 'recent European crisis and outbreak of war' and were convinced that 'the immediate demands on the Development Fund will in all probability be largely increased'. Yet in the next Report they commented: 'the effect of the war on the sphere of the Development Commission has, so far, belied immediate expectations'.

A significant reason for this lack of impact, if thus it can be termed, lay in the Commission's circumscribed powers under the Act of 1910. As 'enablers', to use the modern phrase, they were limited by the flow of applications and where no suitable organisation existed to co-ordinate effort in a particular area of activity, their power to act was at best uncertain. Having said that, the Commission soon realised that a way forward was for it to encourage such associations – the Tobacco Growers Association was an early case in point. In the early days, however, this way forward had yet to be fully realised. It was only later, from the early 1920s, that this fostering of non-profit organisations which could effectively take action indirectly for the Development Commission, was to be properly developed.

In another sense, however, the Commissioners themselves, and presumably their advisory staff, can be held to blame. All through the Minutes of these early days the reader is impressed at the level of detail and thoroughness of the discussions and the constant reference to the limits of the Commission's power. Commissioners seemed almost paranoid about exceeding their authority. In particular they were adamant that they were not to be seen as providing a form of unemployment relief – rather a curious view bearing in mind the commitment which Lloyd George, Churchill and others had given to the whole issue of unemployment. As a result they must frequently have argued themselves out of action which they could have taken. A case in point relates to the key question of home-grown food production. At the sixty-first meeting (8 June 1915) discussion on a report on the position of agriculture after the war prepared by Hall and Wilmot was postponed, 'pending the consideration of a more comprehensive question, namely "THE INCREASE OF HOME GROWN FOOD SUPPLY" [*sic*]'. Lord Selborne, the President of the Board of Agriculture, had been invited to give his views to the meeting. This was surely an opportunity for the Development Commission to come forward with a bold plan which could be effected in tandem with the Board of Agriculture – Hall and Middleton again. Instead Sidney Webb pedantically questioned '... whether the increase of the home food supply was the business of the Development Commission as such'. And thus it was lamely decided that 'members of the Commission might make suggestions upon the subject as individuals'.

Thus a major opportunity was lost and the message was not lost upon Lord Selborne. In August 1916 Prime Minister Asquith had appointed a Sub-Committee of the Reconstruction Committee with Selborne as Chairman, and with Hall (now Sir Daniel) in membership. The Report of the Sub-Committee in 1918, by which time Hall had left the Commission, barely mentions the Development Commission except in passing. References were made to the programme of research and education but, amazingly (considering that Hall was a Sub-Committee member), the credit for the scheme was given to the Board of Agriculture. On the encouragement of the sugar-beet industry the Commission's role was recognised, but the limitation regarding profit-making associations is emphasised with the proposal that either the Act of 1910 be amended or funds be found from elsewhere. The only Commissioner to appear as a witness was Jones-Davies and he reported only on the condition of Welsh agriculture and never once mentioned the Commission.

The final evidence of the limitations which, both self-imposed and visited upon them, hindered the Commissioners can be found in the income and expenditure accounts. Both the Minutes of meetings and the Annual Reports show that Commissioners were continually obsessed with the amount of money in the Fund. There is frequent reference to the uncertainty of future funding and a worry that the Fund would prove insufficient for all the demands upon it, particularly bearing in mind that they viewed many projects as being long-term investments. There were endless calculations as to how much would be needed to replenish the Fund and the end of March 1915, when the original vote of annual money was deemed to come to an end, remained a worrying spectre. Accordingly, the Reports to Government emphasise an apparent financial insecurity, presumably in an attempt to prepare the ground for future income injections. Indeed in the year 1911-12, following Treasury lobbying, no less than £1,500,000 was voted at once on the grounds that the need was pressing.

At one level the Commissioners could hardly be criticised for the care they took over every application. Each was examined in detail, with frequent reporting back and referrals for mature consideration. Yet the Commission, for all the breadth of its brief, seemed frequently reluctant to put at risk the trust given to them as guardians of public money. And so the paradox emerges of a body for ever emphasising the enormity of the task in front of it yet always very significantly underspent.

The historian Jose Smith, in her 1972 study of English social policy in the period 1886-1914, *Unemployment and Politics*, is quite damning in her indictment of the Development Commission's early record. She views the Commission as 'the most conspicuous failure of Liberal unemployment policy' (p. 357) and she is equally scathing about its failure to promote schemes of economic development. The underspending on the Fund provides evidence to support her case. Had the Commissioners been more adventurous and spent moneys as imaginatively as they did with agricultural research and education, then they would undoubtedly have achieved much more. Yet her assessment is one-sided. The Commission's caution reflects the fact that this was a period in which the state was taking its first hesitant steps into matters relating to welfare, economic development, science and education. Furthermore, the Commission was still in its infancy, with a very small number of staff and mainly part-time Commissioners. Finally, it could be said that the judgement was premature. By 1918, as the next chapter will show, there were the beginnings of what were to be major developments in rural industrial support and in rural community development. These two areas were, in later years (and indeed up to the present time), to take over from agriculture as the central activities of the Development Commission's work.

2

Innovation and change 1919-1947

CHAPTER 4

Into the second decade

The publication of the Tenth Report of the Development Commissioners for the period ending in March 1920 provided an opportunity to look back on the first decade of operation. Their view was generally one of some satisfaction and the Report went into much detail regarding the wide range of work which the Development Fund was supporting (Fig. 4.1). Others apparently shared their satisfaction, especially (and with good reason) those with a commitment to agriculture. The *Journal of the Ministry of Agriculture* for March 1921 reported on:

> '...an arresting record of scientific development [which showed] that in all directions research is moving forward towards its goal and that the practice of farming is being quickened and revivified by the devoted work of men and women who give all their energies to the solution of the special problems entrusted to their care ...What this means in the re-population of ... England and to the proper adjustment between urban and rural areas may be left with safety to the smallest imagination.'
> (VOL. 27, PP 1088-9)

The irony here of course, was that much of that same 'arresting record' would in due course be partly responsible for further depopulation of the countryside.

Yet, as the previous chapter showed, the 'arresting record' was not one of total success. It is interesting to note that the major rural policy developments of the Great War – the Milner Committee Report in October 1915 relating to increasing home food production; the creation of county War Agricultural Committees; the boost to home production spearheaded by Prothero (and Daniel Hall) at the Board of Agriculture from 1916; the *Corn Production Act* of 1917 – had all moved forward with little involvement or mention of the Development Commission.

Despite this apparent disregard by some elements of government, money continued to be allocated to the Development Fund, even in times of financial stringency – as in the early 1920s. Explanations for the survival of the Development Commission into its second and third decades can perhaps be seen as having four components. Firstly, as noted above, the Commission, whatever its failures and missed opportunities, was undoubtedly doing good work and any expenditures made were clearly done with the utmost probity and care. Indeed this care in considering applications to the Development Fund appears to have been meticulous arguably to a fault. By the end of March 1935, by which time the Commission had been operating for a quarter of a century, some £9 million had been expended. With some pride the twenty-fifth Report, probably drafted by the new Secretary, E.H.E. Havelock, noted the existence of no fewer than fifty-one volumes, totalling around 11,000 foolscap pages, of reports and records of deliberations.

Secondly, there is no doubt that many, including those in government departments, saw the Fund as being 'useful'. Put bluntly, it provided a source of money which was additional to their normal

Fig. 4.1 The pattern of work after ten years, taken from the Tenth Report of the Development Commissioners, 1919-1929

CONTENTS.

General.

Agriculture and Rural Industries.

(Fig. 4.1 continued) The pattern of work after ten years, taken from the Tenth Report of the Development Commissioners, 1919-1929

Agriculture and Rural Industries—*continued.*

(Fig. 4.1 continued) The pattern of work after ten years, taken from the Tenth Report of the Development Commissioners, 1919-1929

v

Fisheries and Fishery Harbours.

APPENDIX.

Parliamentary allocations. Not quite perhaps a goose with golden eggs, but something like it. In particular, the Board of Agriculture, which became the Ministry of Agriculture in 1919, obviously viewed the Development Fund in this way, a situation which can only have been helped by the presence of the old team (albeit in reversed roles) of Hall (now Secretary to the Board of Agriculture) and Middleton (who became a Development Commissioner in 1919).

Thirdly, the Commission was obviously deeply entrenched in the Establishment. Its membership had, by 1920, not changed a great deal since 1910. Thus the Development Commission could look for support, not just from government departments which enjoyed its largesse, but also from the 'great and good' of Society. The fact that its objectives were firmly linked to the welfare of the rural economy and, thereby, indirectly to the landed interest, only served to increase the value of this position. The tremendous growth in public interest in the English countryside in the 1920s and 1930s seen, for example, in the writings of Stanley Baldwin and the founding of *The Countryman* magazine, also served to entrench the position of the Commission as an agent operating in an important and valued arena. The Scots and Welsh (and the Irish until 1921) with their own representatives on the Commission were also not likely to complain, at least so long as they felt that they were getting their share of the Development Fund.

The final reason for the survival of the Commission lay in the fact that, whether consciously or not, it was able to find new areas of work which were to grow in importance. In particular, from the early 1920s it expanded its work in two areas which were to prove central for decades to come. These were in the development of rural industries and crafts and in the social and community development of the countryside. Commissioners also realised that, because they themselves were unable to take direct action but could only fund and encourage other parties, they needed to create agents to effect their policies. To a limited extent this had happened in the first ten years: the Tobacco Growers Association was an example, albeit one which failed. From the early 1920s the Commission was much more pro-active in working with such agents and in creating them where they did not exist. This was, in fact, to be the essential way of working for the Commission for the next six decades.

The establishment solidity represented by the Commission was augmented by another characteristic of membership – longevity. Most remarkable of all was the Chairman, Lord Richard Cavendish, who remained in that position until his death in 1946. Another of the original Commissioners, Jones-Davies, remained until 1936. Two Commissioners appointed in 1919, T.H. (by now Sir Thomas) Middleton and the Earl of Shaftesbury, were to stay in post until 1939 and 1948 respectively, the latter becoming Chairman for a short while. Another appointee, Dr W.G.S. Adams, who was to become especially significant in the field of social development, joined in 1923 and continued until 1949. The staff of the Commission was no less resilient in the length of time during which members held office. The first Secretary, H.E. Dale, had left in 1919 when he was replaced by his assistant, R.T. Warner. He in turn retired in 1933 and was succeeded by his assistant, E.H.E. Havelock, who continued in post until 1955.

These long periods of service are not just a curiosity, for they bear upon the work of the

Commission and particularly on its approach to that work. At the level of Commissioner it is clear that these men (there were to be no women until after World War Two) got on well and, one would guess, in a 'clubbable' way developed a comfortable *modus operandi* over many years. The influence of the two secretaries, Warner and Havelock, was of at least equal importance. In the recording of advice to Commissioners and in the very phrasing of the Minutes of meetings can be gauged the care and concern for protocol and mature deliberation, supposedly characteristic of the classic public servant. Few errors of judgement were ever likely to be made, but by the same token there is often a suspicion that risk-taking was most definitely to be avoided.

The fact that the Development Commission commenced on a novel programme of rural development from around 1920 can again be at least partially explained by personalities. Chapter 3 noted the appointment in March 1912 of Vaughan Nash to replace Sir Francis Hopwood. The next year he became Vice-Chairman but could spend relatively little time on Commission work in the early years because of his other governmental duties, especially his role from 1916 as Secretary to the Cabinet Committee on Reconstruction. With the war over, he was able to turn his attention to the work of the Development Commission, most notably in the new areas of economic and social development. Thus, just as in 1910 Daniel Hall had championed the cause of agricultural research and education, so ten years later would Vaughan Nash champion other key areas, which would become a major focus of Development Commission work.

The provision of moneys to support fisheries research, to aid the development of inshore fisheries and the improvement of harbours, continued as a relatively minor activity of the Commission up to, and indeed beyond, the Second World War. In the years up to 1924 expenditure was quite high and accounted for about one third of the total budget. This reflected the need for repair and replacement to harbours and fishing fleets which had arisen through war-time damage. Thereafter expenditure, typically, was around ten to twenty per cent of the annual budget. The general failure to bring forth schemes for land reclamation and drainage, which was noticed in the previous chapter, continued during this inter-war period. In several years in the 1930s there was no expenditure at all under this heading and in most other years there was but nominal spending of a few hundred pounds.

The greater part of the expenditure from the Development Fund, generally seventy to eighty per cent of the total in its second and third decades, was accounted for under the general heading of 'Agriculture and Rural Industries'. In practice, this meant essentially three main areas of work. First there was the maintenance of the research and education initiatives. Indeed (although, as will be seen, there was to be very significant changes in the structure and organisation of agricultural research from the early 1930s), this expenditure head would still account for most of the spending throughout the period and beyond the Second World War. The other two areas – the support of rural industries and rural social development – were new, although their development had been foreshadowed during the war. These last two areas of new work are considered in subsequent chapters.

Agricultural research and education

Though Hall had resigned from the Commission in 1917, he remained as Chairman of the Commission's Advisory Committee on Agricultural Science. The dominance of agricultural research in particular, in the first decade of the Commission's work, inevitably provided an impetus into the second and third. Existing research stations had to be funded and new ones still to be created. Thus a horticultural research station was set up in Cambridge in 1923 (later to be moved to Wellesbourne in Warwickshire) and the Hannah Dairy Research Institute was founded at Auchincruive in Ayrshire in 1928. In general, the Commissioners were obviously content to allocate a large proportion of the Fund in this way, although support was not always unanimous. In 1925, at the May meeting of the Commission, Sir William Haldane questioned whether the taxpayer was getting value for money from the substantial support of agricultural research. He was especially concerned that the cost of publication was too high and, at this and subsequent meetings, continued to ask whether more effort should be put into investigations, which would have a more direct and immediate benefit to ordinary farmers. It was left to Sir Thomas Middleton to defend the *status quo* and Sir William's advice seems to have had little influence.

In 1921 the *Corn Production Act* of 1917, which had provided guaranteed prices for cereals during wartime, was repealed. Whether this amounted to a 'great betrayal' of the farming community is still disputed by economic historians. The immediate significance of the repeal for the Development Commission was that Parliament voted an additional £850,000 to the Fund under the compensation arrangements in the Act. The clear view was that this money should be seen as 'coming from the farmers', and it was therefore proper that it should be allocated to agricultural education and research. Accordingly, a 'Special Fund' was created within the overall Development Fund accounts, which was expected to operate until it was exhausted in 1927.

The creation of the Special Fund from the 'windfall' money of the repeal of the *Corn Production Act* allowed the Commissioners to restate the objectives of the Fund, in the particular area of agricultural research and education. The 'chief objects' of the Special Fund were enunciated in the Thirteenth Report as:

- additions to land and improvements to buildings in the research institutes
  and the agricultural colleges;
- the provision of additional local advisory officers;
- help to local authorities in the provision of agricultural education;
- the provision of scholarships for the children of agricultural workers;
- the endowment of a Chair in Animal Pathology at Cambridge;
- the development of a scheme for the improvement of the livestock
  industry and especially poultry.

Some other new areas of work were also forthcoming, including experiments with tractors. Of at least equal significance was the creation, early in 1923, of an 'Agricultural Economics Service', which was to provide economic guidance for farmers and which was, in effect, an extension of the early work on farm costings carried out at Oxford by Orwin. Here again can be seen Hall's influence. Though essentially a natural scientist, he had, early on, shown an interest in the economics of farming. While at Rothamsted he had also acted as advisor to the Guinness farms in Sussex, where he had been especially concerned at the need farmers had for proper financial information. His former pupil Orwin had, as noted, developed this work and it was only logical that it would eventually move to become a national advisory service. An initial payment of £2,000 was made for 'part of the academic year 1922-23', and units for the new service were set up at the university centres in Cambridge, Leeds, Reading and Wye. Thus was created what was to become the Provincial Agricultural Economics Service and which still exists at these and other centres as the Farm Business Advisory Service.

A further scheme was an extension of one which had existed since 1911 – the provision of scholarships, nominally for 'agricultural workers'. In practice, this term was obviously applied in a catholic way. There was a scheme for those who were actually involved in the practice of farming. Class II scholarships were for both men and women wishing to take two-year ordinary diploma courses in agriculture; and Class III scholarships were for one-year (or shorter period) courses at farm institutes. However, neither of these elements proved much of a success by way of demand. In some contrast, a scheme for Class I scholarships was instituted to fund applicants at undergraduate and, more commonly, postgraduate level in the universities. One of the first recipients (1922/23) was Edgar Thomas, later professor of agricultural economics at the University of Reading. Other future scholars of this scheme, which continued throughout the 1920s and 1930s, included Gerald Wibberley, Ireson Selman and Edith Whetham, all of whom became well known in their chosen fields.

Changes and criticisms

In addition to these new initiatives in research and education, there were changes happening that were to have profound implications for the work of the Development Commission. In the first place there were new objectives in agricultural research, which did not have their origin with the Commissioners. In 1926 money from the John D. Rockefeller Foundation provided funds for animal science research at Cambridge and Edinburgh. Again in 1930 the Macaulay Institute for Soil Research was created in Aberdeen, following the bequest in 1928 of £27,000 from Thomas Macaulay, the President of the Sun Life Insurance Company of Canada whose father had emigrated from Scotland.

A second important development was the creation of the Empire Marketing Board in 1926, to encourage in particular the marketing of Empire produce. From then on the Development Fund would no longer fund research in areas which had 'Imperial purposes', since the new Board was expected to look to the existing research stations and commission its own research where this was seen as improving marketing arrangements. The Development Commissioners welcomed this change and did not, apparently, see it as a threat to their own activities. They felt that the extra funds available could but help the course of agricultural science, though they worried that the research actions might become overburdened with work in the process. An Imperial Agricultural Research Conference was held the following year, and a further development was reported in 1929 when, following the Conference, it was agreed that eight Imperial Agricultural Bureaux would be formed, each with a specialised area of research of relevance to agriculture in the Empire. Thus bureaux were created at the existing research stations, such as Rothamsted (soil science), the Rowett (animal nutrition) and East Malling (fruit production).

A further development related to the broader area of state-supported scientific research generally. Medical research had been controlled though a Medical Research Committee from 1913, with the Committee becoming a Council in 1920 under the direction of a committee of the Privy Council. In 1915 a Committee of the Privy Council for Scientific and Industrial Research had been created, followed in 1916 by the formation of a Department of Scientific and Industrial Research. The work of the Geological Survey and of the National Physical Laboratory was transferred to the new Department. It became obvious to many (though perhaps not to the Development Commissioners themselves) that the funding of agricultural research was becoming both anomalous and muddled.

By the end of the 1920s it was becoming increasingly clear that the situation must change and that there was a real need for a properly constituted body, which would have an overall responsibility for the promotion of agricultural research in the same way as existed, for example, for medicine. Up to then the Ministry of Agriculture and Fisheries in England and Wales and the Department of Agriculture for Scotland might make proposals as to research developments, as indeed could other parties. The Departments also administered the grants for the chosen research using moneys granted from the Development Fund. The research stations, some of which at least had become world-class in the quality of the science which they were performing, were also capable of acting, if not with full independence, at least in often innovative and fruitful ways. British agricultural research was certainly eclectic in its structure and operation, but it was not necessarily efficient and streamlined.

In September 1929 a Committee on Agricultural Research Organisation was set up under the chairmanship of Sir Warren Fisher. This reported in April 1930, recommending that an Agricultural Research Council be created to provide the necessary professional advice and co-ordination. The Development Commission was still seen as a necessary component in the agricultural research scene, since it would continue to provide money from the Development Fund. Moreover, both the Chairman and the Vice-Chairman (the latter by now Sir Thomas Middleton who had succeeded Vaughan Nash in 1929) were to be members of the new Council and it was to share accommodation with the Development Commission at Deans Yard, Westminster. The Agricultural Research Council was formally established by Royal Charter on 23rd July 1931.

The Development Commissioners generally welcomed the new Council. However, the Minutes of meetings, while acknowledging the discussions going on in other places, imply that Commissioners perhaps failed to understand the potential significance of the development. In response to a paper tabled at the 172nd meeting in November 1930, noting the proposal to establish an Agricultural Research Council, Lord Shaftesbury commented that 'it seemed to him that there would not be very much left for the Commission to do', but he was answered that there was much other work and, in any case, the Commission was still very actively involved in supporting agricultural research.

To an extent this assurance was true. As has been seen, large sums were still annually granted from the Fund to research institutes and the like. And, as just noted, the Commission and the Council shared both premises and some staff, as well as having some common membership. This last connection was augmented when Sir William Dampier, the first Secretary of the Agricultural Research Council, became a Development Commissioner in 1933. These arrangements, both of funding and of symbiotic working arrangements were, indeed, to continue until as late as the mid-1950s.

And yet the reality, though apparently not really recognised by Commissioners, was that the Development Commission's function regarding agricultural research had become, over the years, something of a fiction. While Commissioners saw their continuing involvement with agricultural research as performing a central role, in reality the Commission was regarded in the main as a useful 'bank' from which much-needed funds would flow. A meeting in March 1932 recorded the views of the May Committee, which had been reported in the previous July to consider the dire state of national finances. Commissioners noted with some surprise that:

> 'The Report contained criticisms due to the fact that a large proportion of the expenditure of the Departments of Agriculture and Fisheries is financed by grants from the Development Fund and ... it was held that the existence of large appropriations in aid tends to lessen criticism on the Departmental Votes'.
>
> (TWENTY-SECOND REPORT OF THE DEVELOPMENT COMMISSIONERS, 1931-32)

Commissioners were further disappointed that the Committee had questioned the level of expenditure on Scottish fishing harbours. In the first instance, they countered the criticism by saying that this arrangement meant that the spending of public money was in fact twice accounted for. In the second, they clearly believed that the importance of their investment in harbours – 'the property of impoverished authorities' – was simply not grasped by the May Committee. The Commission, nonetheless, had to respond practically to the call for economies and so the original expenditure estimates were reduced from £710,000 to an actual expenditure of £560,000. Support for agricultural research was reduced by five per cent.

The Treasury, however, continued to question the level of expenditure and the arrangements for the Development Fund. In 1933 the Commissioners felt they had again to emphasise the value of their contribution by reiterating the story of the established system of agricultural research support. The scheme outlined by Hall in 1910 was still held up as the model. There were now twenty-six institutes in the main subject areas which he had identified. This was all, they argued, 'the result of a considered policy', which should not be upset by short-term expediency. The system had worked well up to, and including, the creation of the Agricultural Research Council (which last they had somewhat ingenuously claimed in their previous Annual Report as effectively their own creation). But then:

> '...(and within a month of the first meeting of the Agricultural Research Council) there came the financial crisis, and there is now the perplexing problem of securing steady growth in a living and hitherto active "organism" on supplies which, for a time at least, must be narrowly restricted...'
>
> (TWENTY-THIRD REPORT OF THE DEVELOPMENT COMMISSIONERS, 1932-33)

As the 1930s progressed, the Annual Reports still gave details of financial support to agricultural research stations and to university and college departments, but they were much reduced from the detail of earlier years. Other agricultural matters were given more prominence, especially if they were linked to unemployment alleviation.

Support for the Land Settlement Association to encourage the settlement of the urban unemployed; schemes for allotment provision in association with the Society of Friends (Quakers); and an Agricultural Camps Committee to provide casual labour for beet, potato and fruit picking enterprises, were three examples. The truth, however, was that the Development Fund had, in practice, done its job by way of agricultural research and education. Funds would still be disbursed but the leading role was in the hands of others.

Final proof, if such were needed, that this was so was to come in a 1938 Report on Agricultural Research in Great Britain produced by the organisation, Political and Economic Planning (P.E.P.). In a wide-ranging review of the whole structure of agricultural research, the Report did not mince its words in giving its assessment of the place of the Development Commission. Whilst recognising its pioneering role, the comments included the view that 'The Development Commission is a purely administrative body' and that 'It should, perhaps, be explained that the Development Fund is now a fiction'. The Report concluded that 'The removal of the Development Commission from the agricultural research scene of what is really a piece of superfluous ...property...', was highly desirable.

The onset of the European crisis and of the war served to delay the implementation of this proposal but it was, nonetheless, an inevitability. Fortunately, Lord Shaftesbury's worries of 1930 that little would remain for the Commission to do were to prove unwarranted. The inter-war years had also seen the development of new and important ways of working.

CHAPTER 5

Developing rural industries

At the fifty-seventh meeting in January 1915, the Commissioners considered an application to the Development Fund from the British Toy Association. The sum of £2,600 was requested, to be used for a period of six months to pay the wages of home workers. The request was rejected, mainly on what might be termed welfare grounds, and the views of Sidney Webb were obviously influential in reaching this decision:

> 'Mr. Webb express the opinion that the cottages of the rural labourers were not suitable for home industries ... It was considered further that the kind of work proposed for the home workers, such as pasting squares on the sides of wooden cubes, was not such as should be assisted from the Development Fund, and that the grant should be refused on the grounds that the nature and conditions of work proposed were not satisfactory.'
> (MINUTE OF FIFTY-SEVENTH MEETING, JANUARY 1915)

This consideration of an application to support rural industries which were not directly linked with agriculture was rare in the early deliberations of the Commission. Commissioners were aware that the Act of 1910 gave them some discretion to fund 'any other purpose' but they were unwilling to go too far, not least because Section 6 of the Act did set limitations. As late as 1920, when the Tenth Annual Report was published, the account of support for 'rural industries' (Chapter VIII) made mention only of flax, tobacco, sugar beet, fruit preservation, cheese making, poultry keeping and other industries closely connected to farming.

Towards the end of the War, J.L. Etty conducted an enquiry for the Ministry of Reconstruction into support for rural industries, mindful of the employment problems which would be faced by returning soldiers. The enquiry concluded that 'the ground is as yet far from clear for laying down any general policy of State aid' in this area. Development Commissioners disagreed with this rather dismissive judgement and held the view that rural industries had potential, not least because of a synergy with arable agriculture.

Etty's report had discussed the need for some form of central body to co-ordinate and support the existing organisations concerned with rural industries. He had, moreover, suggested that the resources for this initiative might come from the Development Fund. Commissioners took the hint and from then on a more decisive approach to rural industry support became evident. They were further encouraged in this direction by the provisions of the *Ministry of Agriculture and Fisheries Act* of 1919, whereby county councils were given the duty of 'formulating schemes for the development of rural industries and social life in rural places'. Following the passage of this Act, a Rural Industries Branch within the new Ministry of Agriculture and Fisheries was created, under the direction of Sir John Green. The Branch's brief was to liaise with county councils and to give commercial advice. Sir John, writing in the *Journal of the Ministry of Agriculture* in April 1920, argued that 'The best remedy [for current inefficiencies in rural industries] is the production and co-operative disposal of a larger range of marketable commodities', and he also emphasised an important role both for 'cottage women' and for 'women of education and reduced incomes'.

The Development Commissioners were aware of the activities of the new Branch in the Ministry and were, therefore, under further pressure to be seen to be doing something for rural industries on their own account. Their starting point was characteristically methodical and cautious and was based on the commissioning of two research studies. A grant of £4,210 was made to the Oxford Agricultural Economics Research Institute, to provide information on the economic prospects for rural industries. The first report on *Rural industries round Oxford* was published in 1921 and had been researched by Katherine Woods. Further research by Miss Woods and colleagues at Oxford was carried out in other regions. In these reports she argued for co-ordination in rural industry support and also stressed the need for skills training, marketing and access to information. A 'Central Advisory Committee' was, it was argued, needed to perform these tasks.

The second study requested by Commissioners looked at experience and practice on the Continent. A fee of £1,006 for this study was agreed to be paid to E.C. Kny, an engineer of Danish birth and Czechoslovak nationality, at the Commissioners' meeting in March 1921. Kny's Report of September 1921 went into considerable detail about German practice, but also considered experience in France, Switzerland, Belgium and Czechoslovakia. Whilst drawing lessons which might be applicable in Britain, Kny was careful not to overemphasise the point: 'It is not my purpose to set up what has been done abroad under one set of conditions, as an example to be followed by the English race, whose genius differs so profoundly from that of the Teuton, Latin or Slav peoples.' His conclusions broadly paralleled those of Woods. He proposed the creation of an 'Intelligence Agency' which would advise on:

(a) the economic possibilities of establishing new industries hitherto carried on abroad,

(b) the revival and extension of existing rural industries,

(c) commercial subjects, including market intelligence, foreign competition, methods of organisation and propaganda,

(d) technical matters, including designing, processes, costing, facilities for training, etc.,

(e) the decentralisation of urban industries which owing to economic causes might more profitably be conducted in the country.

A second proposal in the Kny Report concerned the creation of a 'Co-operative Trading Society' to provide raw materials to rural craftsmen and to market the products. The Society would link closely to the Intelligence Agency and to those groups involved with rural industry, such as firms, Women's Institutes and ex-servicemen's settlements.

A new agency

The Vice-Chairman of the Commission, Vaughan Nash, was especially enthusiastic regarding the development of the rural industry work. It is evident from Minutes and reports that it was he who encouraged his fellow Commissioners in this direction, using his wide circle of contacts to gain outside support.

Action based upon these research reports followed. An advisory committee, chaired by Lord Ernle and with representatives from Scotland, Wales and the relevant Ministries (Agriculture, Labour, Health and Pensions), was set up to advise the Commission on the creation of an agency to provide the necessary information to interested parties. The result was the creation of the Rural Industries Intelligence Bureau in October 1921, with Ernle as its first Chairman. Commissioners approved the granting of £2,500 to fund the Bureau for the first year, and appointed Kny as Adviser to the Commission on rural industries and Director of the Bureau, though he was only to remain in the post until the next year. A 'technical adviser' post was created and held for several years by George Marston. He was subsequently to become the Director of the Rural Industries Bureau in the 1930s. Marston had been the artist on two of Shackleton's expeditions to the Antarctic, and his artistic background was to be repeated in other appointments to the Bureau.

Trustees of the Bureau were appointed from the Ministry of Agriculture and the other departments which had been represented on the Advisory Committee. Other trustees were solicited by Commissioners, with Vaughan Nash and Cavendish being especially active in recruitment. Some who were approached refused, including Lord Leverhulme, whose support had been sought because of his commercial expertise. Those that agreed to serve included Professor Adams (then Warden of All Souls, Oxford and soon to become a Development Commissioner himself) and Muirhead Bone, the eminent architectural artist.

The second recommendation stemming from the Kny Report was followed up by the creation of The Country Industries Co-operative Society Limited, registered as a company and expected to act as the trading body for village industries. Its objectives were set out in an article in the *Journal of the Ministry of Agriculture* in September 1922 as being:

'... to carry on the trade of importers, manufacturers and dealers, both wholesale and retail, of or in any material and finished or unfinished articles required by workers in rural industries, and the sale or hiring of machinery, plant and equipment to workers, and the marketing of their productions, and generally to assist in the development of rural industries upon a sound economic and commercial basis.'

Again, trustees were needed and eventually seven appointments were made. Both the trading company and the new Rural Industries Intelligence Bureau moved into premises in Westminster Bridge Road opposite the new County Hall building of the London County Council. The building contained warehouse space and showrooms, where it was expected that exhibitions of rural products would be mounted.

The Rural Industries Bureau (the 'Intelligence' element in the title was quietly dropped in 1923) was to become a major platform for the activity of the Development Commission. As it grew in influence in the inter-war years it effectively took over from agricultural research as one of the two main new areas of activity by which the Commission was known. In financial terms, the commitment to fund the research institutes and the college and university departments still took the lion's share of annual disbursements from the Fund but it was the network of advisers in rural crafts and industries, together with the social and community developments which will be detailed in the next chapter, that increasingly became the public face of the Development Commission.

The early work of the Bureau

During its first year of operation, the Bureau took account of further research on the state of rural industries, carried out in other counties of England and Wales by the team at the Oxford Institute. An important source of information for these studies was the reports made by the Rural Industries Sub-Committees of the County Agricultural Committees which had been created by the 1919 Act. A library of technical information was also developed and a start made in the publication of a series of pamphlets. In its Second Report, for the year ending March 1924 and appearing as an appendix to the Report of the Development Commissioners, the Bureau could list fourteen such publications. The list gives a good idea of the range of activity, as well as giving what appears as a distinctly quaint flavour to the Bureau's work.

Table 5.1. Pamphlets issued by the Rural Industries Bureau, 1924

1. *Village Life and Country Industries*
2. *Straw Ropes and Straw Envelopes*
3. *Peat Firelighters*
    Notes on Hurdle Making by Machinery in North Wales (leaflet)
4. *The Village Blacksmith and his Outlook*
5. *Walking Sticks*
6. *Suggestions and Opportunities for the Rural Wood Worker*
7. *Hand Weaving and Spinning*
8. *Mat Making*
9. *Compressed and Composition Firelighters*
10. *Rabbit Keeping for Fur*
11. *Poultry Feathers (their utilisation in industry)*
12. *Bundled Firewood Manufacture*
13. *Book-keeping for Small Rural Industries*
14. *Costing for Small Country Workshops*

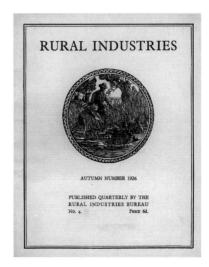

Beyond the series of pamphlets, the Bureau also produced its own journal. Starting in 1925, a quarterly magazine, *Rural Industries*, appeared. Its cover price of sixpence was quickly reduced to twopence in an attempt to increase its circulation among country craftsmen. Its contents were primarily technical, detailing old and new methods, providing patterns, reporting on shows and exhibitions and encouraging the craftsmen to keep proper accounts. It continued in publication until 1939 when war broke out and it was not revived when peace came.

In addition to publications, there was clearly a great deal of practical work going on. A start had been made in giving advice to country wheelwrights, and help to blacksmiths was also a particular area of activity. Linking with the national and county branches of the Master Farriers Association, the Bureau put on demonstrations of acetylene welding. Again from February 1924 an experimental blacksmith's demonstration van, showing 'modern methods and simple machinery' started touring the villages of Oxfordshire. Exhibitions of craftwork were mounted, both permanently in the London headquarters and at regional agricultural shows. Thus was built up a pattern of work, linking advice on craft skills, modern manufacturing methods, design and business advice with attempts to advertise country industry and thus develop markets. This last activity was supplemented by the creation of co-operative associations in the counties, which could provide financial guarantees to members wishing to update their equipment.

The contribution of women to rural industry had been recognised early on. Some observations, at least those from male commentators, were characteristically condescending in their references to the 'domestic industries'. Sir John Green, in his views of 1920 noted earlier, could comment that '... if pleasurable and profitable home work can be given to the grown-up daughters of a family there is less likelihood of the girls leaving home for the urban centres'. There was, however, a much more comprehensive approach taken to involving women. A Women's Advisory Committee was founded in October 1922 with some energetic and influential members. These included Margaret Bondfield MP (who was Parliamentary Secretary to the

Blacksmith's demonstration van, 1923

Ministry of Labour), Mrs Vaughan Nash, Lady Denman and Miss Grace Hadow. These last two, together with Mrs Heron Maxwell, provided a formal link between the Rural Industries Bureau (and thereby indirectly with the Development Commission itself) and the National Federation of Women's Institutes. This organisation, which had been founded in October 1917, had, as will be seen in the next chapter, already benefited from Development Commission funding. Inevitably, perhaps, the focus of the Committee's activity was on 'women's work', such as weaving, knitting, rug-making and pottery. Later on in the 1920s there would be specific schemes to encourage quilting amongst the wives of unemployed miners in Durham and Wales.

A major element of the early work of the Bureau involved co-operation with the appropriate sub-committees of the county councils. Early examples of such co-operation were in the North Riding of Yorkshire and in Oxfordshire, where a Rural Industries Co-operative Society was created in 1923. But it was to be in Kent that this liaison with a 'county council' was to be especially fruitful. As will be seen later, the Kent Rural Community Council had been founded in 1923. By the next year the Community Council, together with the Education Committee of Kent County Council, had been helping the Rural Industries Bureau in the distribution of pamphlets and the collecting of information. It had also shown an interest in the blacksmith's demonstration van and was considering carrying out a survey of rural industries in the county. A year later the Community Council received a grant from the Development Fund to allow it to develop its work into the area of rural industry support. John Whigham Smeal was appointed as the first Rural Industries Organiser.

Smeal remained with the Bureau for many years, later moving (during the Second World War) to become the Chief Rural Officer of the National Council of Social Service for sixteen years. He subsequently became a trustee of the Rural Industries Bureau.

The Commissioners' Report for the year ending March 1925 noted that Kent County Council had delegated its rural industries work to the Community Council. In the next year the Commission provided a guarantee of £500 for two years to enable the formation of the Kent Rural Industries Co-operative Society, based on the Oxfordshire model, so that village craftsmen could re-equip their workshops with modern machinery using instalment credit provided by the Society.

The Ministry of Agriculture had announced in 1925 that no more funds could be expected from them for the conduct of enquiries about rural industries and any subsequent creation of support organisations in the counties. Therefore, the Development Commission had to find an alternative agency to the Agricultural Committees of the county councils. Kent had effectively pioneered this role for its Rural Community Council, and since there were by then thirteen Community Councils in existence, with others nearing formation, the way forward seemed obvious. The choice of the Rural Community Councils as the main agents on the ground for the Bureau's activities was endorsed in February 1926 by a governmental statement on agricultural policy, with the promise that 'The Government will do all in their power to further and support this movement'. In the early stages of this link there were some criticisms that the Commission was showing undue favour to those counties which had Rural Community Councils. Their reply was that some method of rationing funds would have to be employed in any case and that new Community Councils could expect to take on industrial advice work in due course.

Thus by 1926 there had begun a pattern of funding which would be in place for many years. In the year 1926/27 around £9,000 was spent by the Commission under the general head of rural industries. Roughly half (£4,848) went to the Rural Industries Bureau headquarters, which had now moved to new offices in Eccleston Street, Victoria (where it had the rather whimsical telegraphic address of 'Ruritania'). The remainder went in grants of £300-500 to eight Rural Community Councils and three Rural Industries Co-operative Societies, which operated under the auspices of the Rural Community Councils. A further £1,665 was granted to the National Federation of Women's Institutes to aid handicraft work.

By 1931 the Commissioners could look back on ten years of work in rural industry support. By then around £10,000 was spent annually in this way and, while recognising that this sum was but a small proportion of the Commissioners' outgoings, the perceived importance of the work required a review. At some length, therefore, the Commissioners recounted in the Annual Report the creation of the Bureau and the trading organisation, Country Industries Ltd, together with the development of the 'branches' in the Community Councils which were employing rural industry advisers. The Bureau and the Community Councils were clearly seen as the core of the activity. Reference to the trading company was slight, with Commissioners seeming to want to distance themselves from it. It was noted as 'non-official', 'financed from private sources' and 'its formation and its resources were mainly the result of the personal efforts of one of the Commissioners' [Vaughan Nash]. A scheme for the Society to develop a marketing programme on wholesale lines was proposed in 1931 but in the event was not proceeded with. In practice, the trading company proved to be a failure and it was eventually disbanded.

The ten-year review of the Rural Industries Bureau's work was the occasion of some relief by Commissioners. While much had been achieved, there had been times when it seemed possible that the whole venture would fail. In particular the very people whom the Bureau wished to help, the country craftsmen, often appeared unconvinced of the value of the new body. Many were simply reluctant to change their old ways and the problems were compounded by the difficulty of making contact with rural workers, especially in the more remote rural districts. Foreign competition, particularly from American agricultural machinery companies, made life difficult for the village blacksmith. Many craftsmen had naturally based their business on serving the farming community and for much of the inter-war period, agriculture was in decline. And so the Bureau had to encourage them to diversify their products towards other markets. Thus blacksmiths, as well as being trained to work on new farm machinery, were also encouraged to develop wrought-iron work, producing articles for decorative as well as utilitarian purposes. Whether by accident or intent, therefore, the general thrust of the work of the Bureau and its trainers and advisers took on a character emphasising high quality craft and design, rather than more mundane production.

Expanding the Bureau's work

By 1933 the Rural Industries Bureau was operating in twenty-one counties of England and Wales where there were Rural Community Councils. The Bureau felt that there was a need to expand the work, both within and outside these counties, and it was especially keen to expand work on marketing and design. A deputation to the Commissioners came to argue this case in July and the Commissioners agreed to ask Treasury permission to spend an additional £7,000 in this way. Treasury officials agreed, albeit reluctantly. They reported that they felt that the Bureau had been treated very generously in the past and that money for future development should be sought from other areas than just the Development Fund. Throughout the 1930s the Treasury appeared to accept the operation of the Development Commission somewhat grudgingly. However, the Development Commission was generally supported by other government Departments and the Treasury could do little more than send memoranda urging restraint in spending and questioning applications to the Fund. The Secretary, R. T. Warner, and his successor, E.H.E. Havelock, were frequently summoned to the Treasury to discuss these matters.

The bulk of the work of the Rural Industries Bureau was in the English counties, though there was some activity in Wales and in Scotland. In 1929 the Commissioners provided a grant to the Provisional Council for Welsh Rural Development, to encourage rural industrial support in the counties of Monmouth, Glamorgan, Brecon and Radnor. This initiative was especially successful in Monmouthshire, leading to the formation of a Rural Community Council in the county. Four years earlier, in 1925, the Bureau had carried out a survey of the potential of the Welsh textile industry.

Support for rural industries in Scotland was on a much smaller scale than in England, in part at least because there was not the network of Rural Community Councils which could act with the Bureau on the ground. The distance from the London headquarters was also a handicap. Commissioners had granted funds for Bureau work in Scotland during the 1920s and there was some attempt to replicate the English experience. In 1930, a grant of £120 was made to the Department of Agriculture for Scotland for the reconditioning of a blacksmith's demonstration van. However, following the Report of the May Committee on National Expenditure in 1931, even this limited funding was discontinued. Then, in 1933, following a Report to the Scottish National Development Council, it was decided to set up a separate organisation in Scotland to undertake similar work to that done by the Rural Industries Bureau in England and Wales. The Scottish Country Industries Development Trust was formed in 1936 with a grant of £1,600 from the Development Fund for its first year of operation. Funding at a fairly modest level continued in subsequent years.

The Rural Industries Bureau was well established by the outbreak of war in 1939. Its headquarters, which had moved three times since leaving its original base in Westminster Bridge Road, was now in Manchester Square, W1. In addition to the Director (George Marston), a technical adviser and two administrative assistants, there were a draughtsman and advisers in ironwork, textiles, pottery, basketry and quilting. The Development Fund provided in that last year of peace some £31,000 for the support of rural industries. About a third of this went to the Rural Industries Bureau, with the remainder going in the main to the Rural Community Councils to support the county-based advisers in their rural industry work. Modest sums were given to the National Federation of Women's Institutes, and to the Scottish Women's Rural Institutes for the support of handicrafts – and an 'Advisory and Organisation Officer' for the Welsh rural textile industries was also funded through the University of Wales.

Wartime created different conditions for the work supporting rural industries. As the prospect of war grew nearer, the Rural Industries Bureau gave thought to a reorganisation of work which would reflect the greater need to support home food production. The central Bureau staff was increased as was that in the counties. Some peace-time work, such as attempts to improve the marketing of craft products, was suspended as efforts concentrated on agriculture. A particular area of new work developed from 1943 with the appointment of a number of tractor instructors who toured the country, training village smiths in repair and maintenance work. The work of these instructors became more important when American machinery began to be imported as part of the Lend-Lease arrangement.

In June 1940 a Rural Industries Equipment Loan Fund was created with money from the Development Fund. This was initially administered by the National Council of Social Service and was available to craftsmen engaged in repairing agricultural equipment. Use of the Loan Fund was extended in 1942 to potteries and brickyards making land drains, and by the end of the war it was also available to brickmakers, who were seen to be important for the building programme related to post-war reconstruction. The Loan Fund was to continue in one form or another for over half a century.

In May 1940 the headquarters of the Rural Industries Bureau moved yet again, this time evacuating to Taunton in Somerset. Some staff remained in London, though they, too, moved to Taunton when bombs destroyed the London offices in September 1940. By 1943, however, it had become clear that the Somerset location handicapped the national operation of the Bureau. The Commissioners discussed the need for a move back to London at their meeting in March 1943, and offices and workshops in Wimbledon were eventually occupied in 1944.

Wartime also saw the appointment of a new Director to the Bureau. George Marston had died in 1940, just as the Bureau had moved to Taunton. His immediate successor was killed in an accident before he could take up the post and the organisation was leaderless for some considerable time. Eventually Cosmo Clark was appointed in 1942. He was to remain in post for twenty-one years.

Cosmo Clark was, like Marston before him, an artist. In fact he was an Associate of the Royal Academy and had taught at the Slade School. Clark, viewed by many as the most influential Director of the Rural Industries Bureau, brought to the task several qualities which were to influence the work until at least the 1960s, and even beyond. First, stemming from his artistic background, he put a high priority on good design. He would personally vet all new designs and he formed a particularly close association with Edward Barnsley, the celebrated furniture designer.

Cosmo Clark

Barnsley was eventually to become the Bureau's furniture consultant. Clark's concern for quality design and craft skills had a second important influence. He was keen that the advice given to craftsmen was based on real experience and not just on book-learning. Thus, when the Bureau moved back from Taunton to its new headquarters in Wimbledon, he ensured that craft workshops were built where apprentices could come to learn skills they were going to practice.

Cosmo Clark, more than any man, created an ethos for the Rural Industries Bureau which was to pervade its operation for many years. One of his staff who was later to become the Controller of Field Staff, Arnold Pentelow, described the work of the Rural Industries Organisers as 'almost evangelistic'. And Sir Paul Sinker, a future Chairman of the Bureau's successor body, the Council for Small Industries in Rural Areas, could still, thirty years later, describe the work of the Organisers as 'a complicated mixture of commercial samaritanism, advocacy of the parable of the talents and industrial midwifery'. This philosophy was very much Cosmo Clark's creation and it was to colour the economic work of the Development Commission for decades.

The Second World War gave the Rural Industries Bureau a boost in its work and it entered peacetime with some clear ideas as to what was needed in the changed circumstances. The Development Commission had asked G.M. Dykes to carry out a survey of particular rural industries, including the Welsh textile industry, between 1945 and 1946. This linked to efforts to increase the training of new recruits into rural industry, especially in such areas as agricultural engineering. Acting as agents for the Ministry of Labour, Cosmo Clark's idea of a training centre was created at Wimbledon, where trainees spent six months in instruction before being apprenticed to craftsmen in rural workshops. The changes which had been forced upon the Bureau's work by the outbreak of war proved, in fact, to be a more permanent affair than was at first thought. The concentration on helping the agricultural effort would continue in peacetime when post-war policy favoured the support of the farming industry.

By the mid-1940s, therefore, the Commissioners could take some pride in the progress of their innovation of a quarter century earlier. Support for rural industries, by way of advice and training, was widespread in the country areas, and the Commission's creation, the Rural Industries Bureau, had made an important contribution to the war effort. As will be seen next, there could be equal pride in the parallel development in rural community development.

CHAPTER 6

From co-operation to community care

From its earliest days the Development Commission had believed that co-operation amongst farmers was as important a contribution to agricultural development as was scientific research and the encouragement of new crops. In its second year of operation, following discussions with the Board of Agriculture, it had agreed to grant £3,000 to the Agricultural Organisation Society to provide central office staff and a system of training for 'organisers'. The Society had been founded in 1901 to further the development of local associations of farmers and growers for common purchasing and marketing. The Commission continued to fund the Agricultural Organisation Societies operating in England and Wales, Scotland and Ireland on an annual basis although, as was seen in an earlier chapter, their achievements, especially in England, were limited.

The commitment to 'co-operation in agriculture' which had been enshrined in the 1909 Act was, in practice, to provide the vehicle for the Development Commission to become involved in a major way in the support of social and community structures in rural areas. As elsewhere in the progress of the Development Commission's work, there is a paradox here for, while Commissioners continued to stress their focus on economic schemes, they had unwittingly embarked on what was to become a many-sided programme of social development. And again, the explanation for this quite radical new development can be seen in the combination of the commitment of one Commissioner (Vaughan Nash again) on the one hand, and the ideas of some active and imaginative people outside the Commission. The latter had the ideas but they lacked the resources to develop them. The Development Commission could provide those resources.

Approaches to the Commission to fund social organisations in the countryside came from several directions. One was from the Village Clubs Association, then under the Chairmanship of Sir Henry Rew, which had as its main objective the creation of 'village institutes' which would act as meeting places and centres for social activity. A second was to come from the Women's Institute movement which was growing apace.

Even before the formation of the first institute in Anglesey in September 1915, the Agricultural Organisation Society had been persuaded, a little reluctantly, to appoint an organiser to its staff with the object of encouraging the founding of Women's Institutes. This reluctance on the part of the Agricultural Organisation Society to support the institutes grew stronger from 1917 when Leslie Scott (later Lord Justice Scott, who was to chair the Committee on Land Utilisation in Rural Areas during the next war) became its Chairman. His coolness towards the new movement was, however, more than matched by the determination of Lady Denman, who had been appointed as the Chairman of the A.O.S. Women's Institute Sub-Committee in the autumn of 1916. The Sub-Committee asked for funds to appoint more salaried organisers. The Agricultural Organisation Society requested a grant from the Development Commission through the Board of Agriculture, as a separate allocation from its normal support. This precipitated a reaction from the Board which decided that Women's Institutes could not be viewed as an aspect of agricultural co-operation. However, through lobbying by Lady Denman of the Board and its Chairman, Rowland Prothero, it was arranged that a grant of £2,000 from the Development Fund would be paid in 1918 and the administration of the new venture should pass to the Food Production Department of the Board itself. While the Department was abolished after the war, the Women's Institute movement was, thereafter, in a position to look directly to the Development Commission for support.

Beyond the Village Clubs Association and the Women's Institutes, there was a third organisation with a concern for rural social development. The National Council of Social Service had been founded in 1919 to bring together a wide range of voluntary organisations in a federation to eliminate duplication of effort and to present a more unified face to the statutory authorities. A Rural Department was created in November 1919 within the National Council, under the chairmanship of Sir Henry Rew, with the object of encouraging the development and support of voluntary associations in the villages.

Successes and failures

Thus by 1920 there had appeared three main groupings with an expressed interest in rural social development, two of which at least had the makings of a country-wide network of branches. The Women's Institutes were still developing fast and were now approaching the Development Commission directly for funding. Thus in its tenth year of operation (1919/20) the Development Commission was faced with requests from both the National Federation of Women's Institutes and for the Village Clubs Association. It had to make up its mind where it stood on the whole question of the support of social, as opposed to directly economic, ventures.

In the event, and encouraged by the enthusiasm of Vaughan Nash, the Commission recognised the pressure for social development – but only because it persisted in linking such activities with 'co-operation in agriculture'. The Tenth Report of the Development Commissions for the year ending March 1920 records this decision, along with that to award grants of £10,000 to the National Federation of Women's Institutes and £7,000 to the Village Clubs Association. Commissioners

'...had been led to this view by the acknowledged necessity of increasing the amenities of village life as a means of retaining the younger members of the agricultural population who were unlikely, after serving overseas with the colours or working in ammunitions factories at home, to settle down to agricultural life in villages where no opportunities existed for social life or recreation.'

The National Federation of Women's Institutes received a further grant of £10,000 in the next year and £7,250 in the year after. The number of Institutes grew from 770 in March 1919 to 2,323 three years later, by which time federations of Institutes existed in all counties. By then

Commissioners, while very impressed with progress, were minded to limit the level of future annual grants in the expectation that the Federation would become self-supporting. Thus the core grant fell to £4,125 in 1922/23, £2,600 in 1923/24 and just £1,900 in 1924/25. However, funding specifically for handicraft work continued for many years afterwards. From 1925 the Commission began also to support the handicraft work of the Scottish Women's Rural Institutes and it took over the responsibility for providing financial assistance to the Rural Institutes from the Board of Agriculture for Scotland in 1928.

Matters did not go as well with the Village Clubs Association. Only a year after the initial grant of £7,000, Commissioners expressed some concern at the lack of progress, noted the underspending on the earlier grant and contemplated a cessation of grants in future years. They required the Association to match the second grant from other sources on a pound-for-pound basis, to continue co-operation with the National Federation of Women's Institutes and to provide a full report on the working of the Association in October 1921. It was stressed that the grant was for 'propaganda work' to form new associations and that no part of Commission money should be 'applied to the provision of entertainments in villages'. By early 1922, Commissioners were a little more pleased with progress but a further grant was only forthcoming on the condition that no more central staff were appointed. The Commissioners wanted action on the ground. By 1923 any progress by the Association had slowed and a request to the Development Commission to make good any financial deficits was refused. The Association appeared intransigent in negotiation and seemed capable only of holding out the begging bowl. Eventually the Commissioners' patience was exhausted and all support ceased after 1925.

In February 1923 Sir Henry Rew, the Chairman of the Village Clubs Association, had attended a meeting of Commissioners in their Westminster offices. While pleading for continued funding, he explained the failure of the Association to match the success of the Women's Institutes by arguing that the Country Industries Societies, which were being developed by the new Rural Industries Bureau, were 'cutting across' the efforts of the village clubs associations in the counties. Quite how these demonstrably economic organisations could have provided competition to the village clubs, which had predominantly social functions, was not made clear. The irony was that, if there were competing organisations in the offing, by 1923 Sir Henry had already been, though with reluctance, part of the creative machinery which was putting them in place through his capacity as Chairman of the Rural Department of the National Council of Social Service.

Rural Community Councils

A coincidence of events and personalities, starting in early 1919, led to the creation of a network of organisations which was to have a profound effect upon English rural life and, indeed, upon the work of the Development Commission itself. The story of the creation of the first Rural Community Council in Oxfordshire has been told in some detail in Margaret Brasnett's history of the National Council of Social Service. In the first place, Arthur Griffiths was appointed as the rural Secretary for the YMCA in Oxfordshire in the spring of 1919. He quickly developed a programme of instruction and entertainment which was taken to the villages. Then there was Professor W.G.S. Adams, the Warden of All Soul's College, who had recently become involved with the creation of the National Council of Social Service. He had also been one of the prime movers in the creation, in Oxford, of Barnett House as a library and an information centre on social and economic affairs. Thirdly, there was Grace Hadow, a graduate of Somerville College and a former English tutor at Lady Margaret Hall. She had been involved with the Women's Institute movement from its inception in 1915 and had worked with Lady Denman in creating the new organisation. In October 1919 she became the Secretary to Barnett House, largely at the instigation of Professor Adams. In March 1920, Barnett House agreed to the suggestion from Professor Adams that its resources should be made available to people in the Oxfordshire villages. It was Grace Hadow who would be the driving force for making this happen.

The penultimate component in this mixture was to be the involvement of the National Council of Social Service. The Rural Department there was already thinking of ways in which social development might be taken to the rural areas. Inevitably, the Rural Department's Chairman, Sir Henry Rew, favoured the Village Clubs Association. However, perhaps even he could see that the Association was not really in a strong enough position to perform the role, though he pushed its case in a speech at the first conference of the National Council held in Oxford in April 1920. In fact it was Lionel Ellis, the Secretary to the National Council, who effectively involved it in the new venture. He was part of a small *ad hoc* committee which met in the summer of 1920 and which included Arthur Griffiths and Grace Hadow, and also representatives of the University, Oxfordshire County Council and the Workers Education Association. It was this small group which was ultimately responsible for the creation of the Oxfordshire Rural Community Council on 8th October 1920.

One final element remained, and that related, inevitably, to the problem of resourcing the new venture. A successful conference held at St John's College, Oxford, shortly after the founding of the Oxfordshire Rural Community Council, had considered the need to extend the idea nationally. At the Conference were representatives of the Ministry of Agriculture and, importantly in the light of future developments, both of the Carnegie United Kingdom Trust and of the Development Commission. In the first instance it was the Carnegie United Kingdom Trust which, at the request of the National Council of Social Service in 1922, provided £1,000 a year for three years to develop Rural Community Councils. Thus it was possible for councils to be formed in Kent and Gloucestershire in 1923, while others followed a little later in Leicestershire, Nottinghamshire and Derbyshire, all supported by Carnegie money. By 1925 a further seven Rural Community Councils had been founded.

While the Development Commission had been present at the Oxford Conference in late 1920, it had taken no practical part in the movement to create Rural Community Councils. Indeed there is but slight and passing reference in the Minutes of Commission meetings to the new councils in their first few years of operation. In retrospect it may appear surprising that it was to be nearly four more years before there was to be any tangible link formed between the two parties. Admittedly, the Commission felt it had a full programme of work with its long-standing interests in agricultural research and development and, of course, with its new venture, the Rural Industries Bureau. And, as will be seen, there was the customary officer caution.

In July 1924 the National Council of Social Service approached both the Carnegie United Kingdom Trust and the Development Commission for funding for an experimental scheme to provide halls in villages. While some villages had a hall, these were usually where some local benefactor had provided it. Many villages lacked what was seen by the National Council as an important amenity. The Carnegie Trust decided that it could not help this time, and the Development Commissioners agreed, in December 1924, to provide an initial sum of £5,000. The request was viewed as opportune, since Commissioners had by then clearly grown disillusioned with the Village Clubs Association. They felt that the combination of the National Council of Social Service, which would administer the money, and the new Rural Community Councils, which would advise on how it should be used on the ground, was much more likely to deliver results.

The scheme was viewed as an experiment which, if successful, would be extended. The money would be allocated on the basis of interest-free loans providing up to one-third of the cost of a hall. As the Report for the year ending March 1925 said: 'The plan claims no more than to be an attempt to ascertain the minimum amount of public aid required to bring about the maximum result'. If progress was a little slow at the outset – just twenty new halls had appeared by 1928 – the scheme was nonetheless judged a success and it was extended in 1929. Up to then the scheme was only available in counties where a Rural Community Council existed. Thereafter, the Development Commission agreed to open the scheme to other counties where a competent *ad hoc* committee could be formed. Moreover, the Carnegie Trustees decided at the same time that they would be prepared to help in the provision of some halls where Development Commission money was being used. A further £20,000 was added to the village hall loan fund by the Development Commission and the maximum loan was increased to £500. By 1931, 109 new halls had appeared, with applications from a further 168 in process.

In parallel with recognition by the Development Commission of the potential of Rural Community Councils in the provision of village halls, so too was an opportunity seen for them as the local presence in the counties of the Rural Industries Bureau. The lead taken by the Kent Rural Community Council in this regard was noted in the previous chapter.

Following the lead given by Oxfordshire, Kent and Gloucestershire, Rural Community Councils were formed elsewhere such that by 1931 there were twenty-three Councils in operation. Work relating to young people, public health and programmes of adult education were commonly part of each Council's activity, as was advice on local industries linked to the work of the Rural Industries Bureau. Table 6.1 gives examples of the areas of work taken from a list provided to the Commissioners in 1926 by the Kent Rural Community Council.

Table 6.1. 'Typical enquiries actually received at the office of a Rural Community Council'

- 'We want to build a village hall ... can you send some specimen plans and advise us about the Trust Deed?'
- 'Please give me the name and address of the nearest blacksmith who can make me a weathervane for my home, to a special design which I have in mind.'
- 'Please arrange for a visit of the Village Concert Party to this village on...'
- 'Can you help us with advice about starting a boys' club in this village?'
- 'Please send any information you have about schemes for disposing of unburnable rubbish without a charge on the rates…'
- 'Can you tell us where we can get expert advice about the layout of our playing field?'

(SOURCE: DEVELOPMENT COMMISSION PAPERS PRO D4/81)

The range of work was certainly eclectic, though some areas were to be found in virtually all counties. A particularly important area of work, providing services to the parish councils, developed from the early 1930s. Eventually nearly all Rural Community Councils would support the work of a county association of parish councils and it was to prove a major vehicle for their work in the years to come.

The Carnegie money, which had originally allowed the development of the Rural Community Councils, was due to end in 1934. By the early 1930s some of the original foundations were in very serious financial trouble and, indeed, all Councils were hard hit by the cut-back in public funding. Four Councils actually foundered and were closed down. The early funding of Rural Community Councils was frequently precarious and it is probable that, without the Carnegie money, they would never have come about. Certainly it is by no means sure that the Development Commission, though it would in time have a major responsibility to resource the Councils, would have started them.

The main justification for this view relates to the opinions of the Commission's Secretary, R.T. Warner. As in other cases, he urged caution in supporting these new-fangled organisations. In memoranda to Commissioners from 1925 he worried that the Development Fund might be used inappropriately to fund local, rather than national, organisations. He worried also about their rapid growth, and saw the spread of the idea leading to a 'large liability' upon the Fund. Councils, he felt, would be created not because of need but simply because government money was available. His negative and even cynical attitude is summed up in a memorandum sent to Sir Thomas Middleton and Vaughan Nash in October 1925, in which he stated: 'No doubt the work of community councils is largely voluntary, but voluntary work is not always valuable; the movement deals largely in big conferences and definite results are needed.'

Both Middleton and Nash contested this view and a detailed reply from Middleton answered Warner's carpings point by point. Warner, and his successor from 1934 as Secretary, Havelock, who also appears to have had a tendency to parsimony, accepted the Commissioners' view and so the activities of Rural Community Councils grew to be an important element of the Development Commission portfolio. The Annual Reports of the Commissioners from the late 1920s onwards contain detailed accounts of development work in each county, though they tended to concentrate predominantly on the rural industry work and that with village halls. After the Carnegie money had ceased, Commissioners agreed, in 1936, to fund an officer at the National Council of Social Service to develop new Rural Community Councils. They equally agreed to provide some grants to new Councils for core activities where this was not available from other sources, such as local authorities. Under these terms, new Rural Community Councils were formed in Pembrokeshire, Suffolk and the North Riding of Yorkshire.

A concluding assessment

This chapter, and the two before, have necessarily concentrated upon the main areas of the Development Commission's work as it grew and changed during the 1920s and 1930s. The three main areas of activity – agricultural science and development, and the support of rural industries and rural community development – inevitably took up most of the time spent by the staff in the Westminster office. Each of these three activities focused upon a set of appropriate 'agents', for the Commission had no executive authority of its own. Thus the research stations and the universities, the Rural Industries Bureau, the Rural Community Councils, and the National Council of Social Service were the prime direct beneficiaries of the Development Fund. Others, too, benefited, most notably the Women's Institutes, but also, for example, the Land Settlement Association. Then again there was continued support for two other areas of activity which had been there from the very beginning. The construction and improvement of harbours, most notably in Scotland, and support for fisheries research continued throughout this period. The latter activity was guided by an Advisory Committee and grants were given both to government departments and to marine biological stations, some of which were based in the universities.

There were also some individual schemes, which the Commission supported because they linked to its main objectives. Schemes to encourage the electrification of rural areas were seen to be potentially valuable to new rural industries as well as likely to improve living standards in the countryside. Experiments were funded in Herefordshire and in Bedfordshire, but they were not a success. Some schemes were over-optimistic in the estimate of costs while another failed when fraud by one of the employees was detected.

The Twenty-ninth Report of the Development Commissioners appeared in the summer of 1939 as war in Europe was approaching. It was in fact to be the last such Report for twenty-two years. Lord Richard Cavendish was still the Chairman and the list of other Commissioners still included Sir Thomas Middleton, Dr Adams and Lord Shaftesbury. Together these four, by the time they ceased to be Commissioners in the 1940s, had contributed no fewer than 116 years of service to the Development Commission, a commitment probably with few rivals in public service to this day.

Throughout 1945 Lord Richard Cavendish was ill and the Minutes of Commission meetings record his apologies. He died early in 1946 and with him passed an era. Middleton had died in 1943, but Shaftesbury and Adams would continue with the Commission until 1948 and 1949 respectively. Much had been achieved by these men and by their fellow Commissioners since the end of the First World War. Structures which are still existing now were put in place, thanks to the support and foresight of Lloyd George's creation. On the other hand there had been failures and the caution urged by Commission officers probably meant that opportunities had been lost. For all the successes, it is difficult not to get the feeling that the Development Commission needed to change. Certainly the new post-war world would require new approaches and make new demands, not least because new political viewpoints favoured more *dirigiste* attitudes to economic and social development. As the next chapter will show, while the Commission maintained at least some semblance of its long-standing patrician worthiness, a new team, with new ideas, was about to take over.

3

The Albemarle years
1948-1974

CHAPTER 7

Re-focusing the vision

The death of Lord Richard Cavendish created something of an hiatus in the Development Commission. He had been the Chairman for so long, and the pattern of work in its various areas had remained, in structure at least, so consistent over the decades, that the future direction of the Commission seemed uncertain. The social and political environment in the early years after the Second World War was very different from that which had existed in the 1930s, never mind the years before the Great War. The recent war had radically changed both the public and political perception of the role of the state, and the field of rural development was no exception. Rural reconstruction had been put clearly on the post-war agenda, most obviously in a commitment to support home agriculture, but also to produce a planning system which would, above all, protect the countryside from unnecessary urban incursions. Issues of landscape preservation and of the importance of conserving natural resources were beginning to be recognised. A flurry of post-war legislation followed, coming from a Labour government which for the first time could feel confident in its parliamentary majority.

Even before Cavendish's death, the Commission had been thinking, albeit in a rather unfocused way, about its role after the war. At a meeting in September 1943 there was a discussion on 'The future of the Commission'. In fact little was decided beyond the idea that two Commissioners, Professor Adams and the distinguished scientist, Sir Henry Tizard, should go to the Treasury and discuss the Commission's future with Sir Richard Hopkin and Sir Alan Barlow. Nothing of substance was to come of this meeting.

The Scott Report – an object lesson?

By the early 1940s the Development Commission seemed rather to have lost its way and had become to some extent marginalised by the more important players in rural development. The response of the Commission in 1941-42 to the Committee on Land Utilisation in Rural Areas provides an illuminating commentary on this situation and suggests strongly that it was seen by some authorities as stuck in its ways and with an unclear focus of operation.

The Committee, under the chairmanship of Lord Justice Scott, had been created at the end of October 1941 by Sir John Reith, the Minister for Reconstruction, with a wide brief to consider the future of the British countryside. On 28 October Thomas Sharp, one of the two Secretaries to the Committee, wrote to the Commission's Secretary, Mr Havelock, requesting 'a comprehensive, written memorandum of evidence' to be delivered no later than 17 November. A sixteen-page memorandum, detailing in the main the historical development of the Commission's work over the previous thirty years, was eventually produced five months later, at the end of March 1942. The memorandum hardly reads as a bid by Commissioners to have a central role in post-war reconstruction.

Oral evidence to the Committee was given on 30 April 1942 by Professor Adams, Sir William Dampier and Mr Havelock, when Professor Adams argued the need for a central body to overview social and economic research in rural areas. The Commissioners were questioned closely by the Committee's Vice-Chairman, Professor Dudley Stamp, especially on the question of duplication of effort in the support of agricultural research. He had obviously read the P.E.P. Report of 1939. More positively, they were effectively asked the question: 'Is the Development Commission the main national organisation which can drive forward and co-ordinate research, industrial activity and social development in the rural areas?' Havelock answered for the Commission in the affirmative but with his customary caution.

The overall impression given by report of these exchanges is that the Scott Committee was very willing to be convinced of the importance of the Development Commission but that Commissioners effectively failed to grasp the opportunity. A glance at the Scott Report, which followed, shows little reference to the Development Commission beyond brief mentions of the Rural Industries Bureau and the Rural Community Councils. Subsequent meetings of the Commission expressed some surprise at this scant treatment but they must surely have realised that they had lost their chance by their own slackness. There is a poignancy in the fact that one of their own number, Sir Thomas Middleton, had played a significant role in the setting up and operation of the Scott Committee but had clearly chosen to wear his Ministry of Agriculture and Agricultural Research Council hats in so doing, rather than push forward the Commission.

A need to change

On Cavendish's death the Earl of Shaftesbury took the Chair and was confirmed as the new Chairman in October 1946. He was by then seventy-seven years old and, although he was to live on until 1961, was probably already looking to retire from the Commission, which he had joined in 1919. That there was the need for more new blood at the Development Commission was especially clear to the Chancellor of the Exchequer, Stafford Cripps. In early 1948 he had undertaken a tour of the rural areas of Wales and had become convinced of the need to do something to revive the rural economy. Advised by his senior civil servant, Edward Bridges, he sent for the Countess of Albemarle in July 1948 and proposed that she be appointed to the Development Commission with a view to becoming Chairman after a short while. Lady Albemarle had already proved herself in public service, most notably by succeeding Lady Denman as the Chairman of the National Federation of Women's Institutes. She was to be joined on the Commission by three other new Commissioners – John Sullivan, Dr Keith Murray (later Lord Murray of Newhaven) and (later Sir) Jack Longland. What was the beginnings of a new team of Commissioners met for the first time on 1 October 1948 and Lady Albemarle was confirmed as Chairman in the following January, after Lord Shaftesbury's retirement in November.

The Commission needed revitalising but the process was, inevitably, to be a gradual one. In the first place, at least some of the staff at Dean's Yard, where the Commission was still based, were reluctant to change a way of working which had developed over the years. Havelock, who had worked there since the 1920s, had been appointed as Secretary in 1934. The new Chairman's recollection of his reaction to her appointment was that he was courteous to the last, but clearly 'under deep shock'. In her view he had 'run his Chairman' (Cavendish) and the prospect of change clearly did not appeal to him. (She was to add that 'he taught me a bit but he never ran me.')

Secondly, the Commission was always understaffed and its normal duties relating to new funding claims to the Development Fund and its continuing involvement with the Rural Industries Bureau, the National Council of Social Service and all the other agencies and partners which it had accumulated, left little time for many new initiatives. Indeed, the fact that no report on the activities of the Development Commission was published from 1939 until the Thirtieth Report came out in mid-1961 has been quite plausibly explained by the simple pressure of work.

The third, and perhaps most important, reason why progress towards a more dynamic agenda and a revived Development Commission was slow, related to two matters which had been encountered before: financial stringency and Treasury suspicion. The Treasury continued its long-standing practice of questioning the proposals for expenditure submitted by the Commission. From 1951 the matter got serious so that the Chairman had, on occasions, to go to the Treasury in person to argue the case. Commission meetings in this year and throughout 1952 and 1953 discussed the attitude of the Treasury at great length. A proposal from Treasury officials that the Commission should plan to phase out the funding of Rural Community Councils for their work in 'general community activities' led the Commissioners, at their January 1953 meeting, to 'take great exception to this decision' and to send a memorandum to the Chancellor of the Exchequer to request an interview. The memorandum stressed the special nature of the Development Commission and emphasised that it was 'not a normal department of Government'.

This particular spat was settled, and without a visit to the Chancellor, but the battle with the Treasury went on. Post-war financial pressures continued until the middle of the 1950s and the Treasury was obviously annoyed and embarrassed at some of the special pleading on behalf of the Commission, when all other departments of state were being told to economise. It also proposed that certain areas of work might move to be the responsibility of the relevant particular departments. Commissioners, while understandably reluctant to give way too much, realised that they could not be too intransigent and that they very much needed to develop a new momentum to their work.

In the event, the developing confrontation of the early 1950s was generally avoided, although for the first ten years of Lady Albemarle's chairmanship there was an ever-present concern as to survival. This the Commission achieved by a combination of luck and judgement. Financial pressures eased somewhat by mid-decade. The Commission realised that it would be prudent to give way in some areas and to re-group in others. It became clear, for example, that the funding of the construction and improvement of fishery harbours was an area which, albeit with reluctance on the part of some Commissioners, could perhaps be released. Following a meeting with the Treasury in November 1953 it was further agreed that the 'normal and regular work' of the Welsh and Scottish Agricultural Organisation Societies, and of the Scottish Allotments and Garden Society, should in future be funded from the respective departmental votes.

More positively, the Commissioners stressed at their meetings the need to support experimental and innovative work. As will be seen later, this included the encouragement of factory building in some rural areas and, later on, a more targeted response, especially to industrial development in problem rural areas.

Personalities

Of the three other Commissioners appointed with Lady Almemarle in 1948, Dr Keith Murray and Jack Longland were to be especially effective in helping to re-focus the work of the Development Commission. While Murray was to remain a Commissioner only until the end of 1953, he brought some much-needed new thinking to the Commission. Longland, who had been Chief Education Officer for Derbyshire and was later to serve as a Countryside Commissioner and also on the Sports Council, continued the established tradition of longevity, only retiring in 1978.

By 1952 the team of Development Commissioners had changed completely from that which had operated before the Second World War. The Welsh interest was by then represented by Lt Col. Beaumont. He was to prove very active in representing the rural needs of the Principality, especially in the area of industrial development, and was to encourage Commissioners to hold some of their regular meetings at his own house rather than in London. Then there was Leonard Elmhirst. In association with his wife, Dorothy, an American heiress, he had developed a novel experiment in rural development on his own estate at Dartington in Devon. It was he, in particular, who encouraged the Commissioners to mount an annual tour of a rural area to see the problems on the ground. At a later stage, from 1959, the Commissioners were joined by the economist, Professor Ronald Tress. He would be especially involved in the radical transformation of the work of the Rural Industries Bureau in the 1960s.

Members of the Commission's staff were no less influential during this period. Havelock continued as Secretary until 1955 when he was succeeded by his deputy, F.S.O. Broughton. In some ways Broughton continued the tradition of bureaucratic caution, which had been the stock-in-trade of his two predecessors. He is remembered by his Chairman as an intelligent man, but one who was a little distant and even shy. Battles with the Treasury were to be avoided if at all possible.

One further staff member at this time is worthy of mention. Brian Lincoln had joined the staff at Dean's Yard before the war and had rejoined after military service, despite the offer of a more lucrative job in Germany. In 1950 he had moved to work on the staff of the Agricultural Research Council, returning to the Development Commission in early 1952. He subsequently became Assistant Secretary, succeeding Broughton as Secretary in January 1964. In one sense, Lincoln continued a staff tradition as before: by the time he retired at the end of 1974 he had served the Development Commission, or its companion organisation, the Agricultural Research Council, for over thirty-five years. In other ways he was very different. A strong personality with a definite physical presence, he was, to quote Lady Albemarle, 'more of a fighter' than his immediate predecessor, Broughton. Such spirit was to be needed, not least in dealings with the Treasury.

Relationships with government

From its very inception, the Development Commission had always had a sensitive relationship with the various branches of government. The sensitivities were in no way to diminish in the decades after the Second World War. Most directly these relationships were with the Treasury, and the particular difficulties which arose in the early 1950s have already been noted. While the Minutes of meetings at this time make it clear that Commissioners were often irritated by what they saw as unnecessary Treasury interference, it did make them consider the future role of the Commission, if only so that they could better argue their case. Thus, at their meeting in December 1951, Commissioners decided that at some point in the next year they should convene a special two-day meeting to discuss strategic matters, rather than the normal round of considering detailed applications to the Fund.

By May 1953 Havelock could report that he had it on good authority that the Chancellor of the Exchequer had decided on a review of the Development Commission's functions, spurred on, no doubt, by Treasury officials, who resented the 'spending department' behaviour of the Commission. It was deemed prudent to welcome such a review, a sentiment expressed in a letter of 22 May from the Chairman to the Chancellor which, nevertheless, returned to the familiar theme of the special nature of the Commission. By the autumn of 1953 it was reported to Commissioners that, 'The Treasury were under direct orders from Ministers to propose some changes in the scope of the Development Fund'. The report was given by the Assistant Secretary, Broughton, since Havelock had been ordered by his doctors to take a complete rest from work. The strain of Treasury pressure and the impending review was obviously telling on him.

One area of Commission activity, the support of fisheries research, had already been suggested as a candidate for 'hiving off' to another department. While the Commission generally felt that their role here was an entirely satisfactory one, they realised that flexibility in negotiation was needed. Beaumont and Longland were, especially, of the opinion that some long-standing areas of work could be given up and efforts concentrated on new developments. Eventually, in the mid 1960s, this area was to be removed from the Commission's remit and transferred to the Natural Environment Research Council.

This particular battle between the Commission and the Treasury was eventually ended, following a meeting between Lady Albemarle and the Financial Secretary to the Treasury held on 18 November 1953. A more accurate description might be that the engagement was suspended, with skirmishes continuing for the rest of the decade.

Rural Depopulation

Relationships became difficult again in the early 1960s. Commissioners, in seeking a strategic focus for their continuing role, had begun to emphasise the problems arising from rural depopulation, a concern which they felt was central to the original brief of 1910. In November 1960, Lady Albemarle reported to her fellow Commissioners that she had heard informally that an inter-departmental working party on rural depopulation was about to be set up by the Treasury. Any optimistic reaction to the recognition of this important problem (and, by implication, of the Commission's key role in combating it) was to be short lived. The Minutes of meetings held in 1961 record with some pique that the Commission had not been invited to appoint a member to the working party. The Report of the working party was eventually published towards the end of 1961. At this meeting in January 1962 the Commissioners formally received the Report, which had been referred to them by the Treasury. It had, they noted with annoyance, already been accepted by Ministers.

The meeting was clearly an angry one and the Minute recording the discussion extended to more than five pages of foolscap. The Chairman reflected the view of her fellow Commissioners that the failure to consult them on this important matter 'seemed grossly discourteous'. Moreover, they were upset at the comments made in the Report, regarding the powers and activities of the Commission. The Treasury had been especially irked over the previous years by the activity which the Commission had undertaken by way of building factories, especially in Wales (see next chapter). Accordingly, they had asked for a legal opinion as to the extent of Commission powers. The Treasury solicitor had commented on the cumbersome nature of the procedures and, further, that 'it was almost impossible to find a common element in sub-paragraphs (a)-(g) in Section 1(1) of the Act of 1909'. He concluded that, in his view, the Act did not give sufficient powers to the Commission to spend money on building factories.

Development Commissioners reacted by suggesting that this view should be considered by a higher legal authority. Failing a satisfactory response there, then the Act of 1909 should be amended. They were convinced that this latest attack was, as the Minutes recall, 'perhaps a cloak for the Treasury's intense dislike of [the Commission] acting as a spending department and of having to justify expenditure to the Public Accounts Committee'.

Commissioners' criticisms of the Report did not stop there. They felt that, on a topic like rural depopulation, they were the ones with the real expertise. They cavilled at the definition of rural depopulation given in the Report and resented the implication that the Commission's own factory-building programme was an insignificant effort compared with industrial developments carried out by other departments. They criticised the choice of study areas (mid-Wales and Scotland) and stressed their own personal knowledge of depopulation problems in Northumberland and Devon. Professor Tress, perhaps rather curiously, argued that the economic arguments advanced in the Report were too academic. Above all, Commissioners felt that the overall thrust of the Report was towards the *concentration* of new development in larger centres, a policy which contrasted directly with their own efforts at *dispersal* since the late 1940s.

A strongly-worded rebuff was made to the Treasury, countering the comments in the Report. An emollient response to this was considered by Commissioners at their meeting in March 1962, when the Treasury had replied that no discourtesy had been intended. The effect was, perhaps, spoiled by the somewhat sarcastic comment on the Commission's defence of its actions on industrial development that 'here we can only note the Commission's "Apologia pro vita sua"'.

Discussions on the theme of rural depopulation continued at Commission meetings into 1963. Commissioners felt they had at last found in this topic the necessary focus for their efforts – and for their policies of supporting economic and social initiatives in the countryside. They were sensitive to the criticisms that their activities appeared small by comparison with the much grander developments going on at the same time by way of regional planning, new towns and the like. Moreover, Colonel Beaumont had reported at the September 1963 meeting that the reaction in mid-Wales to the Commission's programme was that its efforts were 'puny' by comparison with other governmental initiatives elsewhere.

The discussions on rural depopulation, and the criticisms of the Development Commission's efforts in several quarters, spurred the Commissioners to action. In response to the unsatisfactory inter-departmental report, they had produced their own study of rural depopulation. Originally this had been intended to go to the Treasury but, following a proposal from Leonard Elmhirst at the meeting in November 1963, it was agreed that it would be amended and sent to the new Prime Minister. A Conservative administration had been returned in the October and Sir Alec Douglas-Home had replaced Harold Macmillan as Prime Minister. Inevitably, Douglas-Home immediately passed the paper on to the Treasury.

In fact, this action was to lead to some very significant changes in Development Commission activity. A meeting with Mr Bretherton of the Treasury was arranged, at which there was obviously some productive discussion. While embryonic ideas which Commissioners had had about a policy of concentrating development at certain key points – and following a suggestion from Professor Tress of the need to create a more dynamic 'Rural Areas Corporation' to take over the work of the Rural Industries Bureau – were not discussed, Bretherton did encourage the Commission to argue for an extension, or at least a confirmation, of its powers. Following this, a memorandum on rural development was drafted and considered at the meeting in March 1964. After several attempts at re-drafting, the Memorandum on *Prospects for rural development and redevelopment* was submitted to the Prime Minister (by now Harold Wilson) in October 1964. The Memorandum was eventually published in the Thirty-second Report of the Development Commissioners for the three years ending in March 1965, though this appeared only in July 1966.

Conclusion

The proposals put forward in the Memorandum of October 1964 were to be the core of some radical changes in Development Commission activity, especially regarding rural industrial development. As such, they are the more specific concern of the next chapter. The Memorandum marked the start of a rather more harmonious relationship between the Commission and other parts of government. More significantly, perhaps, the squabbles which preceded its creation can now be seen as a time when the Commission was forced, under attack, to rethink its role and consider more pro-active ways of working. While the Commission's activities in the 1950s were certainly more dynamic than the last years of Cavendish's chairmanship, there was still a tendency to react to grant requests rather than to initiate. The 1960s brought not just changes of government but also different attitudes to state involvement, especially in association with new industrial and technical developments. The Commission may have found the process of enforced change rather painful at times, but in the end it was to create the foundations for what would be, effectively, a real rural development agency.

CHAPTER 8

Strategies for rural industry

In the post-war years the support given by the Development Commission to rural industries continued to be based predominantly on the work of the Rural Industries Bureau and of the Rural Industry Organisers, who were employed by the Rural Community Councils. The war had given a stimulus to this work, notably in the creation of the Rural Industries Equipment Loan Fund in 1940. In 1946 the scope of the Fund was extended to go beyond the provision of equipment for craftsmen and to provide loans for the acquisition of workshops and industrial premises. The Development Commissioners agreed to put £50,000 into the Fund to provide loans for this purpose but, because interest was to be charged on these loans, it was not possible for the National Council of Social Service, as a registered charity, to continue to administer the Fund in the old way. Accordingly, a new organisation was created early in 1947: the Rural Industries Loan Fund Society Ltd. In practice, there was a distinct element of continuity since George Haynes, the National Council's Secretary, became the Secretary to the new Society and administrative services continued to be provided by the National Council.

Loans from the Fund were only available to craftsmen and small businesses employing no more than twenty workers and applicants wishing to borrow money to provide workshops were expected to find twenty per cent of the cost themselves. The maximum loan available was £2,000, with those for premises being paid back over no more than twenty years and those for equipment over a period of no more than five years. While these loans were an undoubted help to rural craftsmen, their usefulness was limited by the credit restrictions which were in place in the post-war years. Indeed, it was not until the early 1960s that these restrictions were eased and the scope of the Loan Fund could be increased. By then around £1.3 million had been loaned from the Fund.

The co-operation of the Rural Community Councils in the work of the Rural Industries Bureau continued. This usually involved the employment of a Rural Industries Organiser and the servicing of a county committee, which provided advice and direction at the local level, including the vetting of applications to the Loan Fund. In general, this relationship appears to have worked well, though there were obvious drawbacks. The Organisers were not employed by the Bureau but by the individual Rural Community Councils. Direct control was therefore not possible and there were certainly circumstances where the independence of the Rural Community Council's chief office led to difficulties. Occasionally the operation of the system may have become a little lax. At their meeting in February 1949, Commissioners discussed a report on the workings of the Loan Fund and were made aware that some officers based in Rural Community Councils were not properly applying the necessary conditions for the receipt of loans. New conditions were accordingly drawn up.

The Rural Industries Organisers in the counties reported on a weekly basis to an Area Organiser. Five Area Organisers covered the country, presenting an immense task for so few people. Thus, the southern Area Organiser had to cover all the counties from Kent to the Isles of Scilly. In the individual counties the Rural Industries Organisers were equivalently stretched. A sample weekly record for Cornwall, for June 1948, shows the organiser travelling nearly three hundred miles in four days, during the course of which he made contact with thirty craftsmen (smiths, wheelwrights, saddlers, carpenters and a rope maker) as well as meeting up with his opposite number from Devon. On Friday and Saturday he did 'office duty' – and did the maintenance on his car. These visits were, as mentioned earlier, the life-blood of the Organiser's work, approached from the 'missionary' viewpoint which had been especially fostered by the Director, Cosmo Clark.

Factory building

The concerns which the Labour government of 1945 had about unemployment were to have important implications for the work of the Development Commission. In particular, there was concern about unemployment in some areas of north Wales and in Scotland. Accordingly, in 1947, after discussions with the Board of Trade and the Treasury, it was agreed that the Development Fund could be used to establish new industries in depressed rural areas. As ever, the Development Commission could have no executive power in this area and so, in practice, it was the local authorities in the affected areas which acted as agents. A policy of building new factories was instituted which was, in later decades, to become a major activity of the Commission. For the first twenty-five years or so, however, this development was on a modest scale and by the early 1960s no more than twenty-two such factories had been built in Wales and Scotland (Table 8.1).

Table 8.1. Factory building in Wales and Scotland, 1947-1961

Wales	Scotland
Pen-y-Groes, Caernarvonshire (2)	Peterhead, Aberdeenshire (5)
Blaenau Ffestiniog, Merioneth (1)	Buckie, Banffshire (1)
Llangefni, Anglesey (5*)	Inverasdale, Ross and Cromarty (1)
Holyhead, Anglesey (1)	Castletown, Argyllshire (1)
Machynlleth, Montgomeryshire (1)	Wick, Caithness (2)
Barmouth, Merioneth (1)	Halkirk, Caithness (1)
Lampeter, Cardigan (1)	

*one factory not taken up

(SOURCE: THIRTIETH REPORT OF THE DEVELOPMENT COMMISSIONERS)

The tentative nature of this initiative may be explained in several ways. Financial restrictions were in operation for much of the time and the Commission felt that it already had a significant economic role through the operation of the Rural Industries Bureau. Moreover, while there was support for the Commission's activities in government, that support was not unequivocal – particularly since some members of government were wary over allowing too much power to an agency involved with local development: they felt this might detract from what was seen as a predominately national approach. There was a national programme of regional planning, based essentially on the *Distribution of Industries Act* of 1945, which had designated Development Areas where new industries were encouraged to locate. These generally excluded the rural areas and it was here that the Development Commission's limited role was seen to be useful.

Beyond these specific explanations for the limited scale of factory development before the 1960s lie some less definite, but nonetheless important reasons. In the 1940s and 1950s the Development Commission, despite the changes in membership, felt nervous about its future in what was obviously a new world. Hampered by this uncertainty and ever mindful of the limits to its executive power, it proceeded with caution. The new factory initiative was dependent upon the small number of requests coming to the Development Fund from local authorities, rather than upon the Commission itself being pro-active and having a defined policy of rural industrialisation which it was keen to prosecute. Beyond the continued support of the Rural Industries Bureau in its long-standing role, the Development Commission lacked a strategic focus for its economic work. There was nothing in the first decades after the Second World War which matched the grand ideas and the strategic purpose which had existed in the early years in relation to creating a system of agricultural research or of rural industry support. These characteristics, of course, reinforced each other. A reactive organisation felt itself to be too busy responding to requests from the Fund to be able to stand back and think seriously about the form of a rural development strategy. And lacking the strategic vision meant that new activities were either rejected or were carried out on a limited front.

Developments in rural Wales

These characteristics of reactivity and the lack of a strategic approach during the 1940s and 1950s can be seen in the Commission's part in rural development activity in Wales. A profusion of reports and plans from a variety of sources appeared in the years after the war, relating to the economic and social problems of rural Wales. A report from the Welsh Reconstruction Advisory Council in 1944 had commented on the beneficial effects of industrialisation. In the early 1950s the Rural Development Panel of the Council for Wales and Monmouthshire came out against a policy to encourage new industry. Then again the individual county councils all had their own views, which were expressed after 1947 in the new Development Plans required by the *Town and County Planning Act* and which, in general, favoured programmes of industrialisation.

By the mid-1950s, the only physical evidence of activity on the ground which had occurred were the few factories which had been funded in part by the Development Commission at the instigation of the county councils. Colonel Beaumont had told his fellow Commissioners that the view in mid-Wales was that the Commission's activities there had been pathetic. At a Commissioners' meeting held at Leonard Elmhirst's home, Dartington Hall, in May 1957,

Beaumont reported further on discussions that he had had with the Secretary of the Welsh Woollen Manufacturers Association, which had been supported by the Development Commission for some years. The Secretary, John Garbett-Edwards, had told him of moves in mid-Wales to create a development agency. A conference under the chairmanship of Professor Beacham, Professor of Economics at University College of Wales, Aberystwyth, had involved representatives of the four mid-Wales counties and had proposed the formation of a Mid-Wales Industrial Development Association.

The Commissioners were uncertain as to whether they should be wary or help the proposed Association, feeling that more research was needed, but at their July meeting they agreed a grant of £500 for three years to help the new agency. The Association was subsequently formed in November 1957, with Garbett-Edwards as its first Secretary. In May of 1958, Commissioners agreed to provide £12,500 to allow the Association to build a factory at Machynlleth. Further lobbying of the Commission by the Association produced funds for an advance factory at Aberystwyth in early 1963, after which the advance factory programme in Wales was expanded to give nine more factories. By the late 1960s, factory development in Wales (and indeed elsewhere) had expanded substantially, but by then the Development Commission had not only become more active in this area but had also begun to think more strategically.

The situation in Wales was admittedly a difficult one. The agricultural lobby was strong and, at least in the early years after the war, it generally opposed industrial development. Then, again, there was political rivalry within local government, which hardly made for concerted action. And the mid-Wales counties generally lacked political clout as compared with the more powerful lobbies in urban-dominated South Wales. So the Development Commission would certainly have been hard-pressed to develop a comprehensive programme in Wales. Nevertheless it is not unreasonable to suggest that, had the Commission then had a national strategy with its associated programme structures and had it felt able to be more adventurous and outgoing in its activities, then more would have been achieved.

Developing a strategic approach

Despite the criticisms which can be made about the Commission's activities in Wales, at least before the 1960s, its experience with factory provision certainly contributed to the development of an economic strategy. The need to define problem rural areas and then to target economic development at particular locations, for example by building advance factories, was obviously one element of this. By the early 1960s, Commissioners were of the opinion that any approach had to be broader than just building factories. In their Thirty-second Report for the period from 1962 to 1965 they could say:

> 'So far as mid-Wales is concerned the point has almost been reached where the provision of industrial premises alone is inadequate and in future it will need to be associated with housing programmes and other services such as training, if people are to be induced to return to an area.'

A second element which contributed in the early 1960s to the development of a more strategic and comprehensive policy was, as noted in the previous chapter, the choice of rural depopulation as a focal theme for the Commissioners' overall approach. As the Commission engaged, not always successfully, in a debate with other branches of government, so it gradually became identified with this particular problem. Moreover, the perceived need to stem population outflow in rural areas encompassed not only employment creation but also policies to maintain and enhance social and cultural facilities – and therefore touched on other areas of the Commission's work. And, of course, the statistics of rural depopulation provided a useful indicator of problem rural areas which might help in the targeting of policies.

During this period Professor Ronald Tress, Professor of Economics at Bristol University and later Master of Birkbeck College, who had been appointed a Commissioner in 1959, had an important influence on Commission policy. Not surprisingly, he took an especial interest in the economic affairs of the Commission. Very soon after his appointment he had visited the headquarters of the Rural Industries Bureau with his fellow Commissioner, C.I.C. Bosanquet. They reported to Commissioners at their meeting in March 1960. When they had asked whether there was a case that rural businesses should pay something towards the national service, the reply was that there would be a concern that craftsmen would respond by reducing their subscriptions then paid to Rural Community Councils. Tress informed the Commissioners that he 'wondered whether there was not a case for the rural industries service being separated from the Rural Community Councils'. Three years later, in September 1963, when the Commission was actively debating the rural depopulation issue, Professor Tress elaborated on this suggestion. He suggested the idea of a 'new Rural Areas Corporation', modelled perhaps on the New Town Development Corporations. Perhaps two new organisations were needed, albeit under the same corporate umbrella: one to 'think' and do research on rural industry problems, and the other with money for action on the ground. In these suggestions can be seen the makings of a radical reorganisation of the work of the Rural Industries Bureau and of the Development Commission itself.

The initial vehicle for the implementation of a more strategic approach was the paper on *Prospects for rural development and re-development* referred to at the end of Chapter Seven. This had effectively been in preparation since late 1963 and was revised during 1964, with Professor Tress being largely responsible for producing the fourth and final draft in October. This paper (subsequently reproduced as part of the Thirty-second Report of the Development Commissioners) strongly argued the need for a 'positive policy for the countryside', because the forces at work in the poorer rural areas were no different from those in the more urban areas, where redevelopment was being actively encouraged, and that the national interest demanded 'the formulation now of a policy for the planned development of regions subject to, or threatened with, rural depopulation'.

Two elements of the new strategic approach were outlined. One sought to continue the general and widespread support offered to local authorities, voluntary agencies and private enterprise where it was requested. The second element was more innovative, in that it proposed the selection of two or three experimental areas (to be known as Trigger Areas) where a more pro-active approach to development and investment would be encouraged. These Trigger Areas would focus on growth points and should be managed by a suitable 'regional association'. The model of the Mid-Wales Industrial Development Association was specifically referred to. Overall, the strategy was apparently modelled on schemes which had been in operation in Norway since the early 1950s but the parallel with current thinking, regarding growth poles in regional development policy generally, is evident.

Three experimental Trigger Areas, in mid-Wales, in the Eastern Borders and in North-east Scotland, were subsequently designated. In these areas a small number of advance factories were built and a programme of development involving the Commission's activities, local government and the voluntary sector was agreed. In practice, of course, the developments in Mid-Wales were a continuation of an ongoing programme and the Development Commission was recognising the pioneering work which had been done there by others. Developments started in the other two areas from 1966.

New building being erected in Market Rasen, Lincolnshire, in 1965

These experiments inevitably attracted some interest in other areas, with the result that the Commission was approached with proposals for similar schemes elsewhere. While these were referred to as 'combined developments', they were similar to Trigger Areas, with programmes of factory construction, employment creation and supporting social policies. The areas were managed by a local association or committee involving the relevant local authorities, the local small industry committees and, in the case of Northumberland, the Rural Community Council.

By early 1973 thirty-five factories had been completed in the Trigger Areas and other chosen areas, with further projects agreed or under construction. The Thirty-third Report of the Development Commissioners (for the period ending in March 1973 but only published a year later) recorded in detail the progress in what were now called Special Investment Areas, a term introduced in the Report. A map (Fig. 8.1) in the Report illustrated the broad areas where factory and other developments were taking place or were proposed and showed clearly that the Commission was moving towards a spatially-targeted policy. Over the next decade and beyond, this approach would be developed further into a formally-designated pattern of Special Investment Areas (and later Rural Development Areas) into which an increasing portion of Development

Commission funds would be channelled. In effect, these designated areas provided the rural match for the larger national pattern of priority areas recognised by regional planning activities.

The Thirty-third Report contained a second map illustrating population changes during the inter-censal period 1961-1971. This showed quite unequivocally that large areas, especially of rural England, had seen substantial population growth in the 1960s. Indeed, the areas defined for local government purposes as Rural District Councils (until 1971) had shown a growth rate of sixteen per cent, or three times the national average. Inevitably this created something of a problem for the Development Commission. It was seen earlier how, seeming to lack a focus for their role after the Second World War, Commissioners had gradually evolved such a focus around the theme of rural depopulation. Within just a few years of this, however, justification for it came into question.

To start with, at least, the Commission could still point to substantial areas of the north and the west where depopulation was still happening. Depopulation continued, therefore, to be used as an important criterion for the designation of priority areas, an approach made rather easier from 1976 when a Treasury report on rural depopulation was published. As time went on, however, and population resurgence spread further and further into the remote countryside, the apparently clear indicator of rural population loss became less and less valid. By the 1980s, as will be seen, it had effectively disappeared as a major topic of interest and concern.

Creating CoSIRA

It was noted earlier that in 1963 Professor Tress had reported somewhat critically to his fellow Commissioners on the operations of the Rural Industries Bureau and had further suggested the idea of a 'Rural Areas Corporation' as a vehicle for the Commissioners' economic policy. Commissioners began to see in this idea the possibilities of a new agency, which would carry economic policy forward and would, in effect, be the active arm of the Commission 'on the ground' with the Commission itself providing the policy thought. A more unified approach to economic and rural industrial development was increasingly seen as necessary. For many years there had been a three-fold approach. The Rural Industries Bureau provided advice and training, the Rural Industries Organisers in the counties (usually in the Rural Community Councils) dealt directly with rural businessmen and craftsmen, and the Rural Industries Loan Fund Ltd, operating under the auspices of the National Council of Social Service, provided finance. The overall impact, though significant, was arguably limited by this profusion of roles.

Just as the favourable response from the Prime Minister to the Memorandum on Rural Development of 1964 had encouraged Commissioners to embark on the Trigger Area experiments, so did it also encourage discussion on creating a more efficient rural industries service. In January 1966 a discussion on the future of the Rural Industries Bureau took place with one of its trustees, Professor Gerald Wibberley of Wye College, present. At the April 1966 meeting of Commissioners, the Chairman reported on the attempts to re-organise the field staff into some form of regional structure. The prospects for this did not seem good, not least because the Rural Community Councils were not enthusiastic about inter-county collaboration. Lady Albemarle

Fig. 8.1

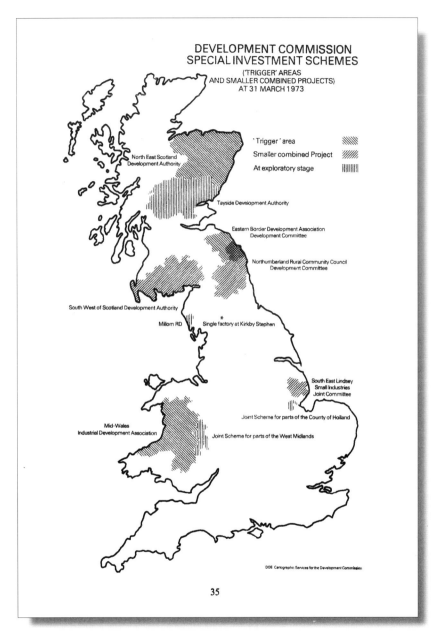

DEVELOPMENT COMMISSION
SPECIAL INVESTMENT SCHEMES
('TRIGGER' AREAS
AND SMALLER COMBINED PROJECTS)
AT 31 MARCH 1973

'Trigger' area

Smaller combined Project

At exploratory stage

North East Scotland
Development Authority

Tayside Development Authority

Eastern Border Development Association
Development Committee

Northumberland Rural Community Council
Development Committee

South West of Scotland Development Authority

Millom RD   Single factory at Kirkby Stephen

South East Lindsey
Small Industries
Joint Committee

Joint Scheme for parts of the County of Holland

Mid-Wales
Industrial Development Association

Joint Scheme for parts of the West Midlands

DOE Cartographic Services for the Development Commission

35

suggested to the meeting that, in the face of these limited attempts at reorganisation, a more thorough-going reform might be needed. A new rural industries organisation might be formed. The title of a 'Central Association of Rural Industries Committees' was suggested.

By the May meeting, Commissioners were clearly moving quite quickly to propose a new structure. Lady Albemarle reported on discussions about making the county Rural Industries Committees independent of the Rural Community Councils. Professor Tress suggested that the

Bureau and the Loan Fund should be amalgamated. The Secretary, Brian Lincoln, was asked to explore these ideas with the Bureau itself and with the National Council of Social Service. It was believed that, while the Bureau would be generally supportive of the ideas (which would, of course, strengthen its overall position), the National Council would be against them.

And so, at least in the short term, it proved. At the July 1966 meeting Commissioners noted the receipt of an 'unhappy' letter from H.S.E. Snelson, the Chief Rural Officer of the National Council. He had written to the Rural Industries Bureau in terms which were described as 'provocative'. Sir George Haynes, the General Secretary of the National Council, was interviewed and asked to explain why the Rural Industries Loan Fund, which he administered, had effectively been closed since April. He explained this by reference to the prevailing uncertainty about the future of the Fund, though there is the obvious suspicion that this had been a rather crude tactic by the National Council to express its opposition to proposed changes.

The opposition to the reorganisation of the Development Commission's economic activities was understandable. Operation of the Loan Fund provided both resources to the National Council for agency services and a locus in the area of rural economic development. Moreover, the Council, and specifically its Rural Department, had a responsibility to support the Rural Community Councils, who also looked likely to lose out. A similar reaction was to be made some years later when the Councils themselves wished to split off from the National Council.

In the event, matters were patched up. Snelson was invited to withdraw his letter while the Commission agreed to form a working party to consider possible ways forward. Commissioners had, however, clearly decided on radical change and discussions continued through 1966 towards the creation of one national body with a secretariat provided by the Commission. At the October 1966 meeting the new body was referred to as a Rural Industrial Development Council but in view of concern that 'industrial development' might give a false impression, Commissioners settled on the definitive name – the Council for Small Industries in Rural Areas.

Lady Albemarle had explained the Commission's thinking to Bretherton at the Treasury in June 1967. He had been supportive and had agreed to recommend the development to Ministers. Yet again the legal incentives of the Act of 1909 appeared as an impediment. The Treasury solicitor had seen 'technical difficulties' in the Commission sponsoring the new organisation. Eventually these were resolved and the development could proceed.

In 1967 the Loan Fund moved from the offices of the National Council to new premises in London and the three parts of the former system were amalgamated under the heading of CoSIRA. The Council was formally incorporated as a company limited by guarantee in February 1968 and the control of the staff of the Bureau passed to the new organisation on 1 April 1968. A Tourism Loan Fund was also created at the same time, reflecting the interest in countryside recreation and tourism which had been growing in the 1960s.

A year before, when the name and structure of the new organisation was still being debated, Commissioners had agreed that a new person should be appointed as Chairman of the new organisation. Lady Albemarle had in mind Sir Paul Sinker, who was due to retire the next year from his post of Director-General of the British Council. Sinker had had a distinguished career as an academic at Cambridge and then in the Admiralty and the Treasury. He was to bring to his new post a clearness of thought which was to prove very valuable to the new Council, which he served as Chairman until he retired in 1976.

Conclusion

CoSIRA was to remain as the economic development arm of the Commission until its activities were absorbed back into the Commission in the late 1980s. Its functions were broadly two-fold: the giving of advice, instruction and management services to small firms in rural areas and the provision of credit services to these firms. It operated under a Council of Management (analogous to the Bureau's trustees) and had a team of field staff who were advised by Small Industries Committees in the counties. In addition, central staff in offices in Wimbledon provided advisory services in management and financial areas and in technical skills such as building, joinery, wrought-iron work, thatching and saddlery. A separate section provided credit services for new equipment, buildings and working capital. The creation of the new organisation proved less of a break with the past than had been intended. The three areas of operation – advice, field operations and the loan fund – remained distinct, albeit within one, not three, organisations. Two subsequent reports on the working of CoSIRA (the Tann Report of 1971 and the Lane Report of 1975) both commented critically on a culture of separateness which they observed in the three operational divisions.

In other ways, however, the creation of CoSIRA marked a very real change. Most obviously it gave a sharper public profile to the Commission's economic work. More subtly, perhaps, it probably made possible a more progressive outlook towards rural industry. The final Annual Report of the Rural Industries Bureau (1967-68) interestingly hints at this change. The review of work reflects the traditional interests in craft industries, like thatching and iron work, and even reports enthusiastically on a 'walking stick forming machine'. The interests of the 1920s and 1930s were still to be found. Elsewhere in the Report, however, there is reference to 'the shape of things to come' – 'This year has seen the first computer installed in a small rural firm'. Increasingly, as the 1970s progressed, the Council would turn its attention from the craft skills to the industries which depended, or indeed were created by, modern technologies of manufacture and the electronic revolution.

The creation of CoSIRA also had the effect of increasing the expenditure from the Development Fund in the areas of small industry support and factory provision. In the final years of Lady Albemarle's chairmanship, the Commission was spending £2-3 million a year in these areas, totals which represented by far the largest proportion of total spending from the Development Fund.

Lady Albemarle retired as Chairman of the Development Commission in May 1974, after nearly twenty-six years in the post. At the outset the survival of the Commission in the new post-war world seemed precarious, not least because some of the older functions had fallen away and no clear focus for new initiatives was forthcoming. The development of such a focus was a long process and when it came, the emphasis given to the problems of rural depopulation might well have been misplaced in a rapidly growing rural world. In practice, however, the real change which secured the Commission's survival, albeit happening gradually and in small scale, was a growing willingness to take a more pro-active stance on matters of rural development, starting with the factory building programme. By the early 1970s, despite some continuing problems, the Development Commission had effectively reorganised its rural economic effort and, as the next chapter will show, had begun to encourage new developments in the area of local and community development. Experience in Wales, in particular, had suggested that, once effective economic strategies had begun to work, then wider horizons opened up involving such areas as housing and training. The scene was thus set for a more dynamic and wide-ranging brief for the Commission, with the prospect that it might develop into a real rural development agency.

CHAPTER 9

Rural communities in a changing world

The uncertainty of direction shown by the Development Commission in the immediate post-war years, which was noted in the context of its economic and industrial activities, was also reflected in its approach to its social and community work. Some of the organisations which it had supported had continued to grow in strength during and after the war, most notably the Women's Institutes movement which, from 1946, was led by Lady Albemarle who had succeeded the first Chairman, Lady Denman. Other organisations, and particularly the Rural Community Councils, were in a more precarious state. Their funding from voluntary sources had fallen dramatically during the war and the financing of the Rural Community Council network was, in fact, to be a major issue for the Commission until at least the beginning of the 1960s. The Councils also had some difficulty in defining their new role in a world where the new Welfare State was seen by some as having completely removed the need for voluntary activity.

The 1940s and 1950s

Towards the end of the war, the Development Commission held discussions with the National Council of Social Science regarding rural community support after the cessation of hostilities. A particular role was identified for village halls which, as before, were seen as crucial to the encouragement of village social life. At least 2,000 villages were reported in 1945 as wanting to build a hall but there were major problems of finance and shortage of building materials. The Carnegie United Kingdom Trust provided £100,000 in 1946 but this fund was exhausted in less than two years. Accordingly, a scheme to provide temporary village halls, often using surplus military buildings, was introduced, using funds from the Ministry of Education and the Scottish Home Department. By 1951 some 157 such halls had been built in England and Wales and a further eighty-five in Scotland. At the beginning of the 1950s the Treasury was persuaded to augment the Village Halls Loan Fund and the programme of hall development could continue on a rather stronger footing.

Support for village halls and for organisations like the Women's Institutes, Young Farmers' Clubs and parish councils were an important element of expenditure from the Development Fund as they had been before the war. However, the bulk of the social and community work which was funded by the Development Commission was inevitably that relating to the Rural Community Councils.

The Development Commission's attitude to the Rural Community Councils in the 1940s and 1950s was a supportive one but, in retrospect, appears somewhat half-hearted. Gradually during the 1950s the funding of Rural Community Councils was put on a stronger basis, but the process was a slow one. The need to support social and community life in the villages, as well as rural industry, was certainly recognised but there had yet to develop the feeling which came later that Rural Community Councils were in some way the 'social arm' of the Commission and, as such, paralleled the Rural Industries Bureau. The role of the Rural Community Councils as the employers of the Rural Industries Organisers was of course seen as important, but other community work was less formally recognised.

There are several reasons which may be suggested for the ambivalence that appears in the attitude of the Commission to the Rural Community Councils during this period. Firstly, the Rural Community Councils were all individual and independent county organisations which were unable, other than through the National Council, to present a unified face to the Commission and thus force the pace. The contrast with the National Federation of Women's Institutes was obvious. Representation to the Commission was thus at second hand through the medium of the Rural Department of the National Council.

A second reason may well have simply been ignorance on the part of Commissioners of the work of the Councils. Once Dr Adams had retired, the pre-war link with the ideology of the Rural Community Councils was lost. A report in July 1954 by Leonard Elmhirst on his attendance at the annual Rural Life Conference makes it very clear that he was generally unaware of the detailed nature of Rural Community Council work. He would have had no direct experience himself from his base at Dartington because a Council was not created in Devon until 1961.

A third reason also emerges from this same report by Elmhirst to his fellow Commissioners. He had specifically had discussions with several secretaries of Rural Community Councils with a view to helping to clarify the Commission's future response. While noting that some officers were doing a 'first class job', he observed:

> 'Equally clearly there were a few Secretaries whose attitude, if taken seriously, might be described as one of sitting in their offices and hoping that the Development Commission were going to guarantee them for life'.
>
> (MINUTES OF 313TH MEETING OF THE DEVELOPMENT COMMISSION, 28 JULY 1954)

The official history of the National Council of Social Service by Margaret Brasnett understandably gives a rather rosy picture of Rural Community Council activity at this time. But it is clear that there was significant variation across the country. Following Elmhirst's report, Lady Albemarle made several visits to Rural Community Councils to see things for herself. At the Commission meeting in December 1957 she reported her findings, which were that some Rural Community Councils were doing little and were taking the financial support from the Development Commission for granted. The Rural Community Councils in Wales were seen as presenting a particular problem by way of inaction and inefficiency. In 1958 Lord Brecon, who was Minister of State for Welsh Affairs, visited the Commission. He commented that his wife knew the Breconshire Rural Community Council – and she was not impressed! Commissioners had recognised this problem in some counties and resolved to have discussions with George Haynes and H.S.E. Snelson of the National Council of Social Service with a view to improving matters.

There were obviously significant examples of excellent rural community work going on in some counties. Indeed Lady Albemarle made this point in her 1954 report to Commissioners, singling out her own county of Suffolk as a particular case. Another notable example was Northumberland, where a Rural Community Council had been formed in 1952. The Northumberland Secretary, Alec Trotter, provided imaginative and innovative leadership from the outset, serving for many years and becoming a well-known and highly-esteemed member of the rural community development world.

The 1960s and 1970s

The partnership between the Development Commission and the Rural Community Councils moved on to a more secure and productive footing in the 1960s. In part this may have reflected a growing national interest in rural matters, especially from the late 1960s when countryside issues appeared on the public stage, as instanced by the 'Countryside in 1970' Conferences. Moreover, there was a developing interest in population growth in rural areas, in the use of the countryside for outdoor recreation and in the whole area of 'countryside planning'. But the change probably also reflected the fact that, as noted earlier, the Commission eventually developed a clearer focus for its activities and social development was seen to have a part to play in that focus.

Sir Paul Sinker (right) visiting an engineering firm in 1968

The first clear sign that the Development Commission was taking a more comprehensive view of rural community matters can be found in the Memorandum, *Proposals for rural development and re-development*, submitted to the Prime Minister in 1964. This Memorandum argued a symbiotic link between the economic health of rural areas and the vibrancy of village social life:

'People will only continue to live and work in rural surroundings so long as they can get what they regard – by increasingly urban standards – as a satisfactory living, with a full range of social services and opportunities for themselves and their families. It follows that, with the numbers sustained by the agricultural industry falling, other employments are urgently needed. Unless plans for new employments are made and strenuously pursued, whole regions – as distinct from smaller areas where decline may need to be accepted as part of a total plan – are likely to suffer depopulation to such an extent that they cease to be viable as economic and social units.'

(THIRTY-SECOND REPORT OF THE DEVELOPMENT COMMISSIONERS, 1963-1965)

Accordingly, in the proposed experiments of the Trigger Areas, social support was seen as an important bolster to, and indeed consequence of, economic growth, leading, it was hoped, to an 'increasingly sophisticated pattern of social services'.

The apparent commitment to rural social support in the 1964 Memorandum should not, however, be exaggerated. And there was an interesting follow-up to the Memorandum. A month after it had been submitted, Bretherton, Under Secretary at the Treasury, came to discuss the paper with Commissioners. While naturally discussing economic matters, and especially the proposed Trigger Areas, he also queried why Commissioners had not put more emphasis on social development. In particular he felt that the changes going on in 'semi-commuter areas' were of especial interest. The Commissioners' response to this mild criticism was that they took the importance of social factors as read. Commissioners did not seem to have picked up the possibility that they could profit from Bretherton's interest, just as years before they seemed to have missed the opportunity provided by the Scott Committee. Years of sparring with the men from the Treasury seem to have made them blind to the idea that a productive and helpful suggestion could come from this direction!

Bretherton was, as the previous chapter indicated, involved later in discussions on Development Commission strategy. He was to contribute again some five years later when, after he had left the Treasury, he was asked by the Development Commission to conduct a review of the work of the Rural Community Councils. Following visits made in the summer of 1969 he submitted his Report to Commissioners, who eventually published it in June 1970 as *The present state and future prospects of Rural Community Councils*. In his Report, Bretherton again emphasised the importance of developments in semi-rural areas – 'I devoted much attention to the attitude of the Councils to work in the "urban fringe".' He recommended that Rural Community Councils should give more time to this area but that it should not detract from the more traditional focus of work.

The Bretherton Report considered other matters, including the issues raised by proposals for local government reorganisation and also some of the ill-feeling present in some counties at the loss of the rural industry work consequent upon the creation of CoSIRA. He also noted the increase in voluntary activity which had developed in the 1960s, especially in the area of countryside conservation – which was to provide an important new area of work for some Rural Community Councils in the 1970s. All in all, his Report was positive in its view of the work which the Councils were doing and he recommended a modest increase in funding, especially in the light of the new areas of work which he had identified.

The late 1960s and early 1970s saw some very significant developments in the activities of the Rural Community Councils, and also some inevitable strains and stresses. They moved away somewhat from their county-based independence and, in 1970, founded a Standing Conference of Rural Community Councils under the auspices of the National Council of Social Service. Thus, not only was there a greater vibrancy and commitment in the work of the Councils, but they were able to see themselves much more as part of a national network. This was to prove the first step towards full independence from the National Council in the 1980s.

Of at least equal significance was the start of the 'Community Initiative in the Countryside' scheme. In December 1971 the Prime Minister, Edward Heath, had emphasised the importance of voluntary activity in a speech to the National Council of Social Service. Following this, Lord Sandford, a Minister in the Department of the Environment, put a proposal to the Development Commission to create new posts in Rural Community Councils, generally known as 'Countryside Officers'. These new appointments, originally made for a three-year experimental period, were expected to engage directly with village communities and with voluntary and statutory bodies, not least in what were seen as important new areas of community development related to conservation and public participation in planning. By April 1974, just before Lady Albemarle retired as Chairman, sixteen Rural Community Councils had been allowed to appoint new staff and more followed during the 1970s.

The boost to rural community work given by these new appointments can hardly be exaggerated. Many of the new Countryside Officers were young graduates and what they lacked in experience they made up for in enthusiasm and energy. In more than one instance, the Chief Officer of a Rural Community Council found his previously rather quiet life suddenly invaded by a young man or woman who was in a hurry to get things done. While styles varied, the new staff introduced a campaigning style into the work of their Councils which had seldom been there before. Some established staff certainly found this new activism disturbing but there was no doubt that it caught the spirit of the times and injected the new blood that these organisations often needed.

Bretherton's concern over rural areas with expanding populations was also to be followed through by the Development Commission. Three studies on the issues raised by 'rapidly expanding rural communities' were commissioned from Rural Community Councils in mid-Hampshire, West Cumberland and in Monmouthshire. They were subsequently published between 1974 and 1976.

Conclusion

The work of the Development Commission in the area of rural social development during Lady Albemarle's time as Chairman splits broadly into two parts. The first, up until the early 1960s, appears as a time of relatively little innovation. The commitments to organisations such as the Women's Institutes and the Rural Community Councils continued in much the same way as it had done before the Second World War. Thereafter, things began to move more swiftly, until by the time a new Chairman was appointed in 1974 the Rural Community Council network could justifiably be seen as a successful and effective organisation and, in general, a worthy deliverer of the Development Commission's social objectives.

4

The English rural development agency 1974-1999

CHAPTER 10

An adaptable instrument of policy
1974–1980

In a speech to a meeting of the Regional Studies Association in July 1975, the Chairman of the Development Commission stated:

> '... in the last year or so, the Development Commission is becoming consciously a rural development agency working, in partnership with local authorities, to a regional plan and on a five to ten year basis of forward costing, with a defined objective of job-creation and support, its leading purpose being to check the depopulation of rural areas'.

In many ways this declaration of the Commission as a 'rural development agency' was wishful thinking and certainly it was premature as a matter of fact. It was, however, characteristic of the new Chairman of the Commission, in that he had a vision for the organisation and was determined to move with all speed towards its realisation. Stating his objective as a *de facto* reality would contribute to this. As he said in the same speech, he viewed the Commission as 'an adaptable instrument of policy', and the subsequent five years were to see adaptation on a substantial scale.

Donald Chapman had succeeded Lady Albemarle as Chairman on her retirement in May 1974. His appointment by the new Labour government (Harold Wilson had defeated Edward Heath in the previous March) was to herald a period of growth in the activities of the Commission which was as speedy as that of its very early years. Within the six years of Chapman's chairmanship, the Commission's factory programme would grow apace, while on the social side the work of the Rural Community Councils in particular would move into a more active phase.

Chapman did not, however, start from scratch. As previous chapters have shown, the last decade or so of Lady Albemarle's chairmanship had provided an essential foundation for new growth. CoSIRA had, despite some early teething problems, increased activity in the field of rural industry support and was already developing a strong public profile. And the same could be said of the Rural Community Councils, where the new-found interest in environmental and conservation issues had given their work a new and popular focus.

The climate of the times

While the personal energy of the new Chairman can explain some of the activity and change of these years, there is also a need to appreciate the political environment of the times within which the Commission had to operate, not least the debates which related to devolution and to public expenditure. This appreciation is perhaps all the more important because Donald Chapman 'engaged' with government in a much more direct way than any of his predecessors, a point which will be returned to in due course.

The Highlands and Islands Development Board had been created in 1965 and had effectively taken over the role of the Development Commission in these areas, though constitutionally the Commission still retained responsibility for the whole of rural Scotland. A growing debate in the 1970s regarding the devolution of power to Wales and to Scotland, which was to re-emerge in the 1990s, had a particular impact upon the Development Commission's sphere of operation. In December 1975 the Scottish Development Agency was set up, followed in January 1976 by the creation of the Welsh Development Agency.

Further to the latter, a Development Board for Rural Wales (effectively paralleling the Highlands and Islands Development Board in Scotland) was formed from 1977. These new agencies were given considerable powers to encourage industrial development, factory construction and environmental rejuvenation, and they were given budgets to match. The Scottish Development Agency also took over the Small Industries Council for Rural Areas of Scotland (SICRAS) which had been established in 1969 by the Development Commission to provide services equivalent to CoSIRA in Scotland.

This devolving of activity from the Commission to national bodies in Scotland and Wales could in some ways be seen as a further example of the loss of responsibilities which had occurred in previous years, as, for example, with fisheries research. On the other hand, it reflected a political reality which the Commission could not ignore. It responded, as often in the past, by re-emphasising its core work and, in this instance, by making a virtue of necessity by proclaiming itself as England's rural development agency. In practice this status was not formally to be recognised until the 1980s, and then under a different Chairman and a government of a very different political complexion. But the foundations were laid in the 1970s, not least by a dynamic programme of industrial investment which emphasised the Commission's role as a rural development agency in all but name.

The political path to full agency status was not, however, to be an easy one. As a contribution to the devolution debate, the Labour government had, in December 1976, issued a consultative document called *Devolution: the English Dimension*. Commissioners responded with their views in March 1977, arguing the case for the Commission to become the English Rural Development Agency, partly on the grounds that this would be no more than a 'fair deal' for England in the light of the new, and well-resourced, agencies for Scotland and Wales. Calculations as to the amount of state money spent per head on the rural populations of the three countries led the Commission to suggest that an annual budget of between £20-30 million would be needed for the task. This contrasted substantially with the level of current advances from the Development Fund of *c.* £7.5 million in the year 1976/77.

A variety of circumstances conspired to delay a change in the hoped-for direction. In the first instance there was some opposition to the agency idea from the local authorities, who saw it as a threat to their own activities in the rural development field. Secondly, the matter became part of a wider debate on rural matters, including discussion on the role of the Ministry of Agriculture and the desirability of a new 'Ministry of Rural Affairs'. Government responded rather half-heartedly to calls for a Royal Commission on the countryside by setting up a Countryside Review Committee, which was predominantly an internal review body. The demands of the Development Commission to be recognised as a fully-fledged rural development agency, perhaps not surprisingly, got lost in the mêlée.

A final circumstance, and probably in reality the most effective reason why there was no action on this issue during Lord Northfield's chairmanship, was the state of national finances. By the time the Commission was making its bid, the Labour government had found itself embroiled in a massive financial crisis, which was eventually to involve the humiliation of an approach to the International Monetary Fund. The time was hardly propitious for a bid from a small rurally-focused government body for a three- or four-fold increase in its budget.

Politics and teamwork

Previous chapters have suggested that the work of the Development Commission frequently reflected the personalities of both Commissioners and staff. This point is no less true of this period, which was to see the productive co-operation of a Chairman and a Chief Officer that was well-attuned to the political environment of the times.

Donald Chapman was a politician, with an academic background in research in agricultural economics at Cambridge, and roots in local government, the Fabian Society and the Labour Party. He had been elected as Member of Parliament for Birmingham Northfield in 1951, a seat which he held until 1970. The year after he became Chairman of the Development Commission he also became the Chairman of Telford Development Corporation. In January 1976 he became a life peer, sitting as Lord Northfield. He possessed qualities which were to explain much of the activity and success of the Commission during the years in which he was Chairman. Firstly, as has already been mentioned, he was a man of action who believed in a 'hands on' approach to his chairmanship. Secondly, he was in harmony with current political ideology, which recognised Labour's traditional commitment to governmental involvement.

Lord Northfield opening the Ashburton Industrial Estate near Ross-on-Wye, Herefordshire, in 1979

Though the Commission's programme of work continued to be implemented in partnership with other organisations, notably the local authorities and the Rural Community Councils, there was a greater sense of *dirigisme* than had been the case before. There followed from this political harmony an understanding of the day-to-day workings of government which had been somewhat lacking before. Moreover, Northfield was helped, especially in the early years, by a good relationship with the relevant Minister, John Silkin, who had originally asked him to take over as Chairman in 1974.

Northfield's political acumen and established contacts were matched in a most effective combination with the new Chief Executive and Secretary to the Commission. Brian Lincoln had retired from the post in December 1974, after nearly forty years service to the Commission. In his place came his deputy, Kenneth Reeves, who had previously worked at the Ministry of Defence. In personality he contrasted somewhat with the ebullience of Lord Northfield, but the contrast made for an effective team. Moreover, as an established civil servant, Reeves knew the way in which government departments worked. If Northfield knew the workings of Westminster, then Reeves knew those of Whitehall.

Expanding the factory programme

To some extent the Commission had been in a state of limbo during the early 1970s. In 1970 they had submitted a memorandum to the government, emphasising the need for a more active rural policy, but it was not until 1975 that any clear response was received back. The eventual catalyst for the response was the study of rural depopulation, which had been produced by an inter-departmental group co-ordinated by the Treasury. The Report was eventually published in 1976 but before that, in January 1975, its conclusions provided sufficient foundation for the new government to give the Development Commission a new remit for action, focusing on the creation of new jobs in areas which were particularly suffering from depopulation.

The Report, and the governmental green light which came from it, provided the Commission with enough justification for a major programme of factory development in particular. In retrospect, however, there is something of a paradox here. At the same time as depopulation was being resurrected as the key indicator of rural problems, so was the evidence mounting that rural population growth was to be the demographic *leitmotif* for the future. Bretherton's interest in 'rapidly expanding communities', which was noted in the last chapter, was to prove a more prescient idea than had been realised.

The Report on Rural Depopulation suggested that a programme of creating 2,500 jobs each year for ten years would be appropriate. Government concurred and saw the Development Commission as the major contributor, in partnership with the local authorities, to this goal, and so, from 1975, the Commission set its own target of creating 1,750 jobs a year. Northfield travelled the country to assess the rural problems himself, encouraging local authorities to join with the Commission in factory and workshop construction. While sometimes initially suspicious, the local authorities in fact responded and submitted the Action Plans which had been requested.

Fig 10.1 Development Commission Special Investment Areas, March 1979

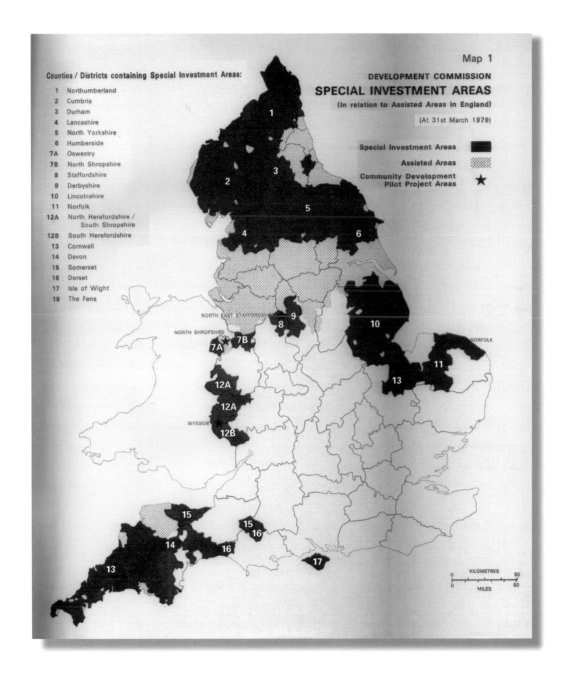

Counties / Districts containing Special Investment Areas:

1   Northumberland
2   Cumbria
3   Durham
4   Lancashire
5   North Yorkshire
6   Humberside
7A Oswestry
7B North Shropshire
8   Staffordshire
9   Derbyshire
10 Lincolnshire
11 Norfolk
12A North Herefordshire /
    South Shropshire
12B South Herefordshire
13 Cornwall
14 Devon
15 Somerset
16 Dorset
17 Isle of Wight
18 The Fens

Map 1

DEVELOPMENT COMMISSION
SPECIAL INVESTMENT AREAS
(In relation to Assisted Areas in England)
(At 31st March 1979)

Special Investment Areas
Assisted Areas
Community Development
Pilot Project Areas

The Development Commission factory and workshop programme of the 1970s was, by any standards, an impressive achievement. While the Commission had first begun to build factories some thirty years before, there had never been a comprehensive programme as such. Accordingly, as was seen earlier, factory development in Wales and Scotland had been *ad hoc* in its provision and very dependent upon the local authorities approaching the Commission rather than *vice versa*. By 1980, and the termination of Northfield's chairmanship, no fewer than 883 factories and workshops had been approved for development, representing over two million square feet of workspace. The factories built in the Special Investment Areas (Figs. 10.1 and 10.2), which coincided with the Government Assisted Areas, were built and managed in partnership with English Industrial Estates, while those in other Special Investment Areas were managed by CoSIRA. By the end of the decade most Special Investment Areas had a quota of factory projects either completed or in progress and factory development accounted for nearly £6 million of expenditure from the Development Fund. Commissioners also recognised that there were rural areas outside the Special Investment Areas which suffered from economic decline. Accordingly they began a programme of designating so-called 'Pockets of Need', where workshops could also be developed.

The development of the factory and workshop programme, both in the Special Investment Areas and in the Pockets of Need, followed the conventional wisdom of regional planning which emphasised the importance of creating 'growth poles' for investment and economic development. Thus Commissioners were keen that CoSIRA field staff integrated their own activities with the area around Commission-funded factories and that there was some coherence with other developments in regional assistance. To this end the Commission coined the rather quaintly-named concept of 'Areas of Pull' – that is the hinterlands around factory developments, within which public and private economic initiatives should be encouraged to link up and co-operate. These Areas of Pull were to be delineated in strategies which the Small Industry Committees in each county were required to produce from 1976.

While the scale of new factory development during the 1970s provides perhaps the most obvious sign of the Commission's economic activity, it was but one part of a broader strategy. As already noted, this strategy involved a deliberate attempt to engage positively with local authorities and it also required a strategic plan to be prepared for each county. A further important element in this comprehensive approach involved the work of the Commission's main agent, the Council for Small Industries in Rural Areas (CoSIRA).

The creation of CoSIRA in 1968 from the three former parts of the Rural Industries Bureau had undoubtedly had some initial problems which had taken some years to overcome, though by the time Lord Northfield became Chairman of the Commission it was generally working well. However, other developments which have already been considered, most obviously the impending withdrawal of Commission activity in Wales and the 'new remit' from government, provided the opportunity for a review of CoSIRA in 1975. Walter Lane, who had been Clerk to Lindsey County Council, was asked to conduct the review of CoSIRA's policies, activities and priorities.

Fig 10.2 Development Commission Factory Projects, March 1979

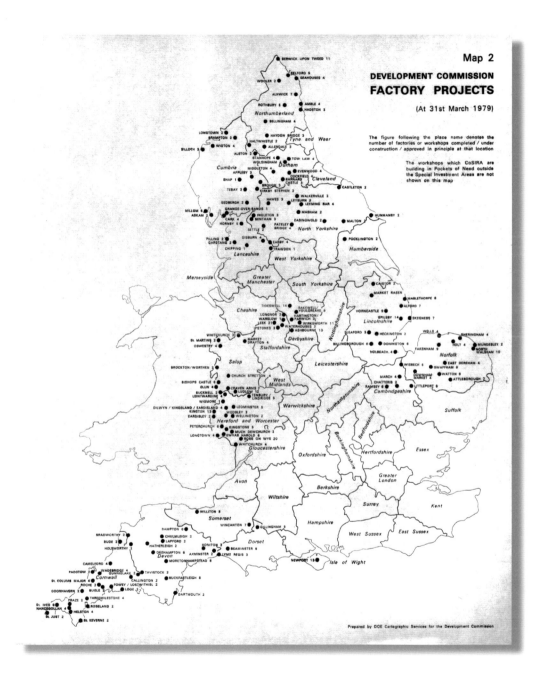

He reported in January 1976 and his conclusions were assessed by a working party of Commissioners, which reported in the following October.

The Lane Report heralded some significant changes in the way in which CoSIRA went about its work and, in effect, it finally removed the last vestiges of the old Rural Industries Bureau. The national economic recession was forcing a stricter control of expenditure and this was most obviously accommodated in setting clearer priorities for CoSIRA activities. Thus, activity was primarily to be concentrated in the Commission's own Special Investment Areas and in the Government's Assisted Areas (Fig. 10.1). Developments outside these areas would take second priority and would be focused on the defined Pockets of Need.

The Lane Review also led to important organisational changes. At the top level CoSIRA's Council of Management was replaced by a smaller Board of Directors, with most members having special responsibility for particular regions. The Chairman, Sir Paul Sinker, retired in 1976 and, for a short time at least, was replaced by Lord Northfield. In May 1977 the chairmanship was taken up by Clive Wilkinson, a Birmingham City Councillor, who became a Development Commissioner at the same time. Below this executive level there were also changes. An executive management team, led by CoSIRA's Chief Executive, was responsible for policy implementation, while Assistant Controllers were appointed at regional level to provide a closer link between the centre and the field staff out in the county.

One final change in CoSIRA activity took place towards the end of the 1970s. As part of a general governmental policy of office dispersal, the intention had been to find a new location for field staff headquarters in either Bath or Bristol, though other sites in Andover and Basingstoke were also considered. In the event no suitable sites were found in these places. Temporary accommodation had been found in Salisbury by Arnold Pentelow, the Controller of CoSIRA's Field Staff Division, and it then proved possible to find a site in the city for a new purpose-built building. Building commenced in 1978 and it was eventually opened in March 1980.

Although the latter years of Lord Northfield's chairmanship were inevitably influenced by growing problems of public expenditure, the record of rural economic development was impressive. Not only was there substantial activity on a number of fronts, most notably factory building and CoSIRA reorganisation, but there also emerged a more coherent policy of strategic planning. Later political ideologies might criticise the dependence on governmental intervention and public expenditure and its adherence to somewhat suspect development concepts, such as growth poles, but there can be little doubt that the 1970s laid the foundations for the higher profile taken by the Development Commission in the 1980s on the developments of the previous decade.

Social and community development

While perhaps less spectacular than the expanded factory programme, activity in social and community development also made significant progress during this period. As before, this area of Development Commission activity focused very substantially on the work of the Rural

Community Councils, with the Commission providing direct core funding to thirty-six Councils in England and also supporting the Rural Department of the National Council of Social Service. Financial support also continued, on a smaller scale, to some of the long-standing beneficiaries from the Development Fund, notably the National Federation of Women's Institutes and the National Federation of Young Farmers' Clubs.

Several factors, which have been noted before and which had started during the time when Lady Albemarle had been Chairman, provided important stimuli to rural community development. As already noted, during the 1970s there was a growth in interest in countryside issues on a wide public front. The activities of other government agencies, especially the Countryside Commission, which had been created in 1968, also served to spur on the interest in rural affairs. And in the universities there was developing a new focus of study, based in part on the revival of interest in rural sociology. This discipline had largely fallen into disrepute until it was revived, if not single-handedly, at least in significant part by Howard Newby, then a young sociologist at the University of Essex, who was later to become a Development Commissioner in the 1990s.

These contextual developments in the national understanding of countryside issues undoubtedly aided the social work of the Development Commission, not least because other government departments were effectively forced to raise their level of interest in rural matters. Two particular aspects of this increased interest are worthy of note. In 1978 the Standing Conference of Rural Community Councils published a report on *The Decline of Rural Services*, based upon research in six counties in the south-west of England. The public reaction to this report was unprecedented, with the number of letters to *The Times* reaching record proportions. In the same year government, through the Department of the Environment, for the first time commissioned a programme of rural research. Issues such as the effects of village school closures and the impact of settlement planning strategies were to be investigated, as was the nature and extent of rural deprivation. This last research study, carried out by Brian McLoughlin at the then Chelmer Institute in Essex, was to have important repercussions on rural policy, not least in the Development Commission, during the 1980s.

A further encouragement to rural community development centred around the continuing success of the Community Initiative in the Countryside Scheme, which had been introduced in 1973. By April 1974 sixteen Countryside Officers were being funded by the Commission on a three-year experimental basis. Ten more counties were allowed to appoint field officers in 1975, by which time the Commission had agreed to fund the posts for a further two years. A review of the scheme in 1977 endorsed the view that it had been highly successful in initiating community activity in rural areas, and by 1979 twenty-eight Rural Community Councils had Countryside Officers in post.

In the light of these developments the Commission launched a review of its rural community development work by its recently-retired Secretary, Brian Lincoln. His report was made available in July 1975. It broadly endorsed the continuing role of the Rural Community Councils and, specifically within this, commented favourably on the Community Initiative in the Countryside Scheme. Some particular problems were also recognised, not least those which stemmed from the reorganisation of local government, which had come into force in April 1974. Rural Community Councils had had to come to terms with new structures, particularly the new District Councils which were frequently unaware of the history of co-operation between Rural Community Councils and local government. Thus, new relationships had to be forged, not least so that funding levels could be maintained.

Significant changes, some of which would only become important in the 1980s, also occurred in the National Council of Social Service. While rural community work had been an important part of the Council's activities since at least the days of Dr Adams, during the 1960s it had tended to downgrade this focus in favour of urban work. Moreover, while a new, often radical, approach to urban community work had appeared during the 1960s, no such change had appeared in relation to rural community work.

Within the National Council, rural staff had been absorbed into a general community work division and the old Rural Committee had been disbanded. By the mid 1970s, however, the National Council had begun to recognise the spirit of the times and the new-found interest in matters rural. Accordingly it re-created a Rural Department in an effort to develop both its service to the Rural Community Councils and to the Development Commission as its advisor on rural social policy.

In 1977 the National Council appointed a new Chief Rural Officer to head up the new Rural Department. David Clark came to the post with a background in academia and in local government, and with an energy and commitment which matched that of Lord Northfield. He rapidly provided leadership within the loose confederation of the Standing Conference of Rural Community Councils which had been created in 1972. With a young and enthusiastic team in his new department, he encouraged the Rural Community Councils to undertake more and exciting work in community development. Above all he was able to publicise the role of the Councils and their work – the publicity engendered by the report on *The Decline of Rural Services* was a notable example of the new style.

Clark's aims were more than just a heightened profile for rural community work, and for the Rural Community Councils, though that was a necessary foundation. He believed in the need for a public presence for the Rural Community Councils, which would match that of CoSIRA within the portfolio of the Development Commission's work. And he wanted to increase the appreciation of rural social issues within the political arena. Inevitably the changes he introduced, especially in the latter area, created a reaction in some quarters. Some Rural Community Councils did not take easily to the suggestion that they should adopt a more 'activist' stance on rural issues, not least because of possible dangers to their charitable status, and they were concerned that their major funder, the Development Commission, might not be wholly supportive of the change.

These two issues – a clearer public face for the Rural Community Councils and the development of a more politicised approach to rural social issues – were to come to the fore in the early 1980s. In the meantime, the social programme of the Development Commission was to expand in other directions and not just within the workloads of the Countryside Officers in the Rural Community Councils. One aspect of this related to the commissioning of research projects, something which the Commission had generally not previously undertaken. In the mid 1970s a number of research studies were carried out by outside consultants, though one, a social study of Millom in Cumbria, was undertaken by the Rural Community Council of Cumbria. Two other studies on rural social issues were commissioned from the Dartington Amenity Research Trust (DART), part of the organisation which had been created by Leonard Elmhirst at Totnes in Devon. A study of Okehampton considered what was needed in a struggling rural area by way of economic and social regeneration, while a second study considered these questions in a broader context of problem rural areas generally. Out of these studies came six pilot community development projects, located in the Wyeside area of Hereford and Worcester, the Staffordshire moorlands, North Shropshire, North Norfolk, Okehampton (Devon) and Caradon District (Cornwall). Three of these projects were carried out under the auspices of the county Rural Community Council, while the others were the responsibility of DART (Devon and Cornwall) and of the North Norfolk District Council.

These pilot studies provided valuable information and experience of what was needed in English rural development. Along with the new activities undertaken by Rural Community Councils, they were part of the foundation of a revival of rural community development theory and practice, which was to come to develop strongly in the 1980s. In the short term, however, their promise was halted by restrictions on government expenditure. They effectively remained as pilot studies despite the wish of Commissioners to expand them into other areas, where they would become a social component to match economic developments in the Action Plans being produced in the Special Investment Areas.

Conclusion

The activity of the Development Commission and its partners during the 1970s, both on the economic and on the social fronts was, in retrospect, remarkable in its breadth and size of operation, particularly bearing in mind the fact that public expenditure constraints were almost constantly present. The Commission had indeed proved itself to be adaptable and, in all but name and legal status, had effectively re-invented itself as England's rural development agency. It had not only expanded its work into new areas but had become very much more pro-active than it had been in the past. In this particular respect the period marked a very real break with tradition.

While some of this activity can be explained by personalities, it must also be seen within its overall political context. Despite the constant, and growing, handicap of public expenditure constraints, the programmes which the Chairman led were, in general, consistent with governmental attitudes. A dynamic partnership between the state and the private and voluntary sectors within a general model, not unlike an urban development corporation, fitted the mould.

Yet soon that mould would be broken. In May 1979 Margaret Thatcher defeated James

Callaghan at a general election, with the result that a Conservative government of a very different political complexion came to power. In the short term Lord Northfield continued as Chairman of the Commission, but his tenure was bound to be limited. A shift in the political paradigm, at least on a par with that which brought in the Liberal government in the first decade of the century, was to occur, which would inevitably affect the workings of the Development Commission in the new decade. What was to prove the penultimate chapter in the history of the Development Commission was about to begin.

CHAPTER 11

Growth and change 1980–1990

Within a few weeks of the election of the Thatcher government in 1979, radical changes in national policy, especially as regards the role of the state, became clear. The future did not augur well for the Development Commission. In the first place it was by definition a purveyor of public funds. There was, it was argued, a clear practical need to assess the level of public expenditure in the light of the catastrophic financial crisis which had faced the recent Labour government and this would inevitably impact upon the transfers into and from the Development Fund.

More significantly the ideological climate had radically changed. The commitment to state *dirigisme* and public funding was immediately challenged, thus threatening the partnerships and initiatives which Lord Northfield had spearheaded during his time at the Development Commission. Moreover, the whole issue of the future role of unelected and potentially unaccountable bodies such as the Commission was being questioned. A general assessment and frequent abolition of the multitude of 'quasi-autonomous non-governmental organisations' ('quangos') was put in hand. The fact that the Development Commission was a body of long and venerable standing, and one with excellent 'establishment' credentials, appeared to be of little significance to a government which was determined to slough off many old associations and alliances.

A review of the role of the Development Commission and its main agency, CoSIRA, was announced in 1980 but the results were not to emerge until March 1982. In fact this review was, in retrospect, simply the beginning of a long period, during which governmental assessments and reorganisation within the structure and operation of the Commission and its partners seemed to be ever-present. These changes were inevitably irksome and time-consuming, particularly for senior staff, but the result was that, by the end of the 1980s, the Commission had undoubtedly emerged as both a *de facto* and a *de jure* rural development agency.

Margaret Thatcher and Lord Vinson at the opening of 'Best Made in the Countryside' exhibition, 1987

But it was not to be Lord Northfield who would see these developments put in place. The shift in the political climate was such that, put bluntly, his face did not fit with the new regime. In May 1980 he was replaced as Chairman by Mr Nigel Vinson, who had become a Development Commissioner in the previous year and who would become Lord Vinson in 1985. Vinson was undoubtedly more in tune with the new political ideologies. He was known to the new Prime Minister, Margaret Thatcher, and was a friend of one of her key advisers, Sir Keith Joseph. A self-made businessman himself, he had developed his own manufacturing process in plastic coatings from scratch, to the point where it had been publicly floated and subsequently sold off. Just as the former Chairman had fitted well into the world of local authority partnership and corporatist linkages between public and private sectors, so did the new incumbent match the new mould which focused upon the private entrepreneur.

Changes also took place in the staffing of the Commission. Ken Reeves, who as Chief Executive and Secretary had developed such a productive partnership with Lord Northfield, retired in July 1981, to be replaced by John Williams, who had been seconded to the post from the Department of Transport. In his turn, Williams developed a close working relationship with the new Chairman. Together they would be responsible for the implementation of major changes of legislation and operation. Lord Vinson, in particular, was determined to heighten the public image of the Commission and to move it towards the role of an advisory agency to government. For this to happen there had to be established a proper publicity machine, so a new communications branch was formed and consultants engaged specifically to strengthen the impact of the Commission's publicity for rural problems. New senior staff were also recruited, itself an interesting comment on the new Chairman's political acumen at a time when jobs in the public sector were being significantly reduced.

Politicising rural issues

The changed political climate of the early 1980s also showed itself in a broader arena than just within the changing personalities at the Development Commission. The interest in rural issues and the future of rural communities, which had grown during the 1970s, began to take on a more overtly political complexion, especially as it became clear that the new government had radical and critical views about the support of public services. Moreover, unlike virtually all its predecessors, Conservative and Labour, it seemed to have no special commitment to the rural areas. The encouragement to a more active espousal of rural interests taking place within the Rural Community Councils, noted in the last chapter, was an important component in the increased politicisation of rural issues. David Clark, the Chief Rural Officer of the National Council for Voluntary Organisations (the new name of the National Council of Social Service), was especially keen to see a stronger public presence from the rural community lobby and he was a prime mover in the bringing together of a number of rural organisations to form the umbrella organisation, Rural Voice, which was launched in November 1980.

Rural Voice, an amalgam of rural interest groups including the farming organisations, the Rural Community Councils, the National Federation of Women's Institutes, the Council for the Protection of Rural England and the National Association of Local Councils, was to prove a significant element in the 1980s in the articulation of rural economic and social issues, especially under its first Chairman, Michael Dower. As a separate, non-charitable organisation it was able to enter the political arena and contribute positively to the national discussions on such emerging issues as rural deprivation and rural housing needs.

In his second Report as Chairman of the Development Commission, Nigel Vinson welcomed the formation of Rural Voice, which he saw as a necessary lobby for rural issues and a body able to take a more outspoken line than the Commission in publicly arguing the rural case to government. While this was undoubtedly true, the welcome hid a nervousness which he, and probably some other Commissioners, felt about the new organisation. In part this was because it might at times steal the Commission's thunder, but there was also a worry that too blatant a critical stance could be counterproductive with the government.

On balance, however, the creation of Rural Voice acted as a support for the Development Commission, simply because it could say things with which the Commission might be in sympathy but about which it felt it, as a part of government, had to be more publicly circumspect. A case in point related to the sale of council houses, a policy proposal which had played an important part in the election of the Conservatives in 1979. The potentially damaging implications of this policy in rural areas undoubtedly concerned the Development Commission and it pushed government to introduce some limitations to its application in rural areas. It was left, however, to Rural Voice and its constituent members, notably the National Farmers' Union, to lead the opposition in the public arena. In practice a valuable two-pronged strategy developed, whereby the Commission was increasingly able to make public statements on rural issues, often paralleling comments from Rural Voice, while at the same time it was able to get its message through privately to ministers because of its close political links with government.

A new legislative foundation

In statutory terms the Development Commission was still constituted under the terms of the original Acts of 1909 and 1910 and it was still at least nominally operating in the old way, by which it recommended expenditure to government rather than disperse its own funds. Technically, all that had changed since the early days of Lord Richard Cavendish, was that the Department of the Environment had, since 1971, taken over from the Treasury as the relevant department of government to which the Commission had to refer. In actual practice, of course, there had been significant changes. In the latter stages of Lady Albemarle's chairmanship, and even more so under that of Lord Northfield, the Commission had begun to initiate developments rather than simply waiting for an approach from another party. Nonetheless, the position had become anomalous and there had been suggestions that CoSIRA had been operating in an *ultra vires* capacity, insofar as it had been aiding profit-seeking private concerns, something which, it will be remembered, had expressly been excluded under the original legislation.

The over-long review of the Development Commission was eventually published in March 1982. The Commission's continuing role was confirmed and it was agreed that it would in future have greater freedom of operation, both to spend its own funds (which would now be given as a grant-in-aid) and to designate its own areas for priority consideration. After seventy years of operation, the Commission was at last to take on an executive role and to become fully accountable for its own decisions and actions.

These new powers had to be vested in new legislation, and to that end a Bill was presented to Parliament in December 1982 by John (later Lord) Wakeham, Minister of State at the Treasury. The Bill was in fact a composite one, designed to encompass a varied collection of financially-related measures. Wakeham, in referring to the existing status of the Development Commission as being to 'advise' how moneys from the Development Fund should be spent, viewed the arrangement as being 'archaic and possibly unique'. At the Second Reading of the Bill, the opposition spokesman, Robin Cook, supported the proposed changes, adding: 'indeed it would be strange if we [the Labour Party] did otherwise'.

Following the referral of the Bill to a Standing Committee, it returned to the Commons for the Third Reading on 12 April 1983, moving to the Lords on the next day. On 9 May the measure was debated in the Lords, having been through its Second Reading on 25 April. At this debate the former Chairman of the Development Commission, Lord Northfield, supported by his colleague Lord Cledwyn, argued for an amendment to the Bill. They were concerned that one clause in the Bill allowed for the Secretary of State for the Environment to direct the work of the Commission, thus removing, in their view, the element of independence from government which had previously existed. They argued that this might result in the Commission becoming the puppet of government and, moreover, that the direction might stifle the support of innovative developments which had been characteristic of the Development Commission's work in the past. In the end, after assurances were given from government that the Commission's independence would not be compromised, the amendment was withdrawn and the clause (no. 8) remained. The *Miscellaneous Financial Provisions Act 1983* was passed on 13 May 1983 and came into force on 1 April 1984. For the first time in over seventy years there was now an actual body called the Development Commission, as opposed to a Development Fund, together with a body of Commissioners.

The Commission thus joined the other two countryside agencies, the Countryside Commission and the Nature Conservancy Council, as 'grant-in-aid' bodies. It was given significant new powers and new responsibilities. Not only was the Commission given executive authority, but it also had a new role as the adviser to government on rural matters. No longer would it simply advise on the spending of moneys from a fund but it now had a duty to 'keep under review and advise the government on matters relating to the social and economic development of rural areas'.

This meant that from now on the Commission could comment on, and indeed intervene, in a much wider range of rural issues than before. It meant also that it could engage in work with other government departments and agencies, with local authorities and, significantly, with the private sector. This new ability to form working partnerships was to be crucial to the new development strategies which were to become central to the Commission's activities from the mid–1980s.

New ways of working

The favourable outcome of the governmental review announced in 1982, and the firmer legislative base provided by the new Act, allowed the Development Commission to look forward with some confidence to the future. In June 1984 it published its prospectus, *The Next Ten Years*, in which it set out its objectives and announced the new areas of priority to be called Rural Development Areas (RDAs). The Commission saw its objectives as threefold:

1. To keep under review all matters relating to the economic and social development of rural England; to advise the Secretary of State on these matters as necessary; and to increase awareness of the problems and needs of rural areas.

2. To strengthen the economy of rural areas in particular by increasing the number and variety of employment opportunities available within them.

3. To ensure that the availability and quality of services, including housing, social and community facilities in rural areas, are maintained and, where possible, improved.

The designation of the RDAs involved a long process of data analysis and public consultation held in 1983 and 1984. The old Special Investment Areas and the Pockets of Need had been chosen in a rather vague way, with rural depopulation being taken as a main indicator of rural problems. In the case of the RDAs the process was a much more rigorous one, and was based on guidelines which had been determined by government. Depopulation was still seen as a useful indicator but unemployment effectively replaced it as the main criterion. In all, there were six criteria recognised and it was expected that all new RDAs would exhibit above average unemployment, along with several of the other indicators. The six criteria were:

1. Unemployment above average for Great Britain.
2. An inadequate or unsatisfactory range of employment prospects.
3. Population decline or scarcity was having an adverse effect.
4. A net outward migration of people of working age.
5. An age structure that was biased towards the elderly.
6. Access to services and facilities was poor.

In all some twenty-eight RDAs were defined (Fig. 11.1). In each RDA a co-ordinating committee was to be formed, involving all the interested parties – County and District Councils, Rural Community Councils, CoSIRA staff and others such as National Park authorities where appropriate – with a first task to produce a Rural Development Programme (RDP) containing both a broad strategy looking forward for five years or more, and a detailed work programme covering a three-year period.

The activities of the Development Commission, and more specifically those of its agent CoSIRA, were in future to be significantly concentrated within the RDAs. Indeed, it was expected that around three-quarters of the Commission's budget, which in 1983-84 amounted to some £23 million, would be spent there. Of the total budget, around half went on the provision

Fig. 11.1 Development Commission Rural Development Areas as designated in 1984, with factory and workshop projects, April 1985

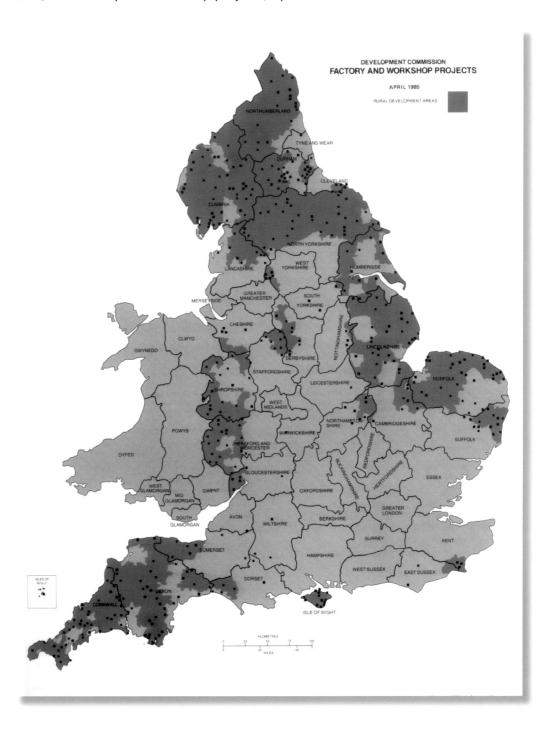

Table 11.1 Development Commission factory and workshop schemes, April 1985

Avon
- ● Peasedown St John

Cambridgeshire
- ■ Chatteris
- ■ Christchurch
- ■ Kimbolton
- ■ Littleport
- ■ March
- ● Wisbech

Cheshire
- ■ Chawley
- ■ Hampton Heath
- ■ Wrenbury

Cleveland
- ■ Lingdale
- ■ Loftus
- ■ Skelton

Cornwall
- ■ Bolhetherick
- ■ Bude
- ■ Bugle
- ■ Callington
- ■ Camelford
- ■ Cligga
- ■ Culdrose
- ■ Doublebois
- ■ Goonhavern
- ■ Grampound Road
- ■ Gunnislake
- ●■ Helston
- ■ Indian Queens
- ■ Launceston
- ■ Liskeard
- ●■ Looe
- ■ Lostwithiel
- ■ Mevagissey
- ■ Mullion Area
- ■ Nancegollan
- ■ Newlyn East
- ■ North Petherwin
- ■ Padstow
- ■ Pensilva
- ■ Porkellis
- ■ Rame
- ■ Roche
- ■ Rock
- ■ St Agnes
- ■ St Colomb Major
- ■ St Dennis
- ■ St Germans
- ■ St Ives
- ■ St Just
- ■ St Keverne
- ■ Stithians
- ■ Stockeclimsland
- ■ Treburley
- ■ Tregony
- ■ Truro
- ●■ Wadebridge
- ■ Warbstow
- ■ Whitstone

Cumbria
- ■ Allerdale
- ■ Alston
- ■ Ambleside
- ■ Appleby
- ■ Arlecdon
- ■ Askam in Furness
- ■ Aspatria
- ■ Bowness
- ■ Brampton
- ■ Brough
- ■ Caldbeck

Cark in Cartmel
- ■ Cark in Cartmel
- ■ Cleator Moor
- ■ Coniston
- ■ Dalton
- ■ Egremont
- ■ Flookburgh
- ■ Grange over Sands
- ■ Greenodd
- ■ Keswick
- ■ Kirkby Lonsdale
- ■ Kirkby Stephen
- ■ Longtown
- ●■ Millom
- ■ Orton
- ■ Patterdale
- ● Penrith
- ■ Penruddock
- ■ Ravenstonedale
- ■ Sedbergh
- ■ Shap
- ■ Silloth
- ■ Tebay
- ■ Threlkeld
- ■ Thursby
- ■ Troutbeck Bridge
- ■ Ulverston
- ■ Wigton

Derbyshire
- ▲■ Ashbourne
- ■ Bakewell
- ■ Chapel en le Frith
- ■ Hartington
- ■ Tideswell
- ▲ Wirksworth
- ■ Youlgreave

Devon
- ■ Ashburton
- ■ Aveton Giffold
- ■ Avonwick
- ■ Axminster
- ■ Bampton
- ■ Bovey Tracey
- ●■ Bradworthy
- ■ Buckfastleigh
- ■ Chagford
- ■ Chillington
- ■ Chudleigh
- ■ Chulmleigh
- ● Cullompton
- ■ Dartmouth
- ■ Hatherleigh
- ■ Hemyock
- ■ Holsworthy
- ■ Honiton
- ■ Ilfracombe
- ■ Ipplepen
- ■ Kennford
- ■ Kingsbridge
- ■ Lapford
- ■ Lifton
- ●■ Lynmouth
- ■ Moretonhampstead
- ■ Nodbury
- ■ North Tawton
- ■ Noss Quay
- ■ Okehampton
- ■ Princetown
- ■ Salcombe
- ■ Seaton
- ■ South Brent
- ■ Tavistock
- ▲ Uffculme

Dorset
- ■ Beaminster
- ■ Bridport

Gillingham
- ■ Gillingham
- ■ Lyme Regis
- ■ Maiden Newton
- ● Sixpenny Handley

Durham
- ■ Barnard Castle
- ■ Burnhope
- ■ Chilton
- ■ Cockfield
- ▲ Crook
- ■ Esh Winning
- ■ Evenwood
- ●■ Ferryhill
- ■ Fishburn
- ■ Lanchester
- ■ Langley Park
- ■ Middleton in Teesdale
- ■ Quarrington Hill
- ■ Sacriston
- ■ St Johns Chapel
- ■ Sedgefield
- ■ Sherburn Hill South
- ■ Hetton
- ■ Stanhope
- ■ Stillington
- ■ Thornley Station
- ■ Tow Law
- ■ Trimdon Grange
- ● Wheatley Hill
- ■ Wingate Grange
- ■ Wolsingham

Gloucestershire
- ■ Cinderford
- ■ Coleford
- ■ Lydney
- ■ Northleach
- ● Soudley

Hereford & Worcester
- ■ Bromyard
- ■ Eardisley
- ■ Ewyas Harold
- ■ Kingsland
- ■ Kingstone
- ■ Kington
- ■ Ledbury
- ■ Leintwardine
- ●■ Leominster
- ■ Longtown
- ■ Moreton-on-Lugg
- ■ Peterchurch
- ●■ Ross-on-Wye
- ■ Tarrington
- ■ Weobley
- ■ Whitchurch
- ■ Wigmore

Humberside
- ■ Carnaby
- ■ Goxhill/Thorton Curtis
- ■ Hornsea
- ■ Howden
- ■ Kilham
- ■ Kirton in Lindsey
- ■ Middleton on the Wolds
- ■ Pocklington
- ■ Sandtoft
- ■ Winterton
- ■ Withernsea

Isle of Scilly
- ■ St Mary's

Isle of Wight
- ■ Freshwater
- ■ Lake
- ●■ Newport

Norton Green
- ● Norton Green
- ■ Ryde
- ●■ Sandown
- ■ Shanklin
- ● Somerton
- ■ Ventnor
- ■ West Cowes
- ■ Wroxhall

Kent
- ■ Appledore
- ■ Lydd
- ■ New Romney

Lancashire
- ■ Barnoldswick
- ■ Chipping
- ■ Earby
- ■ Gisburn
- ■ Hornby
- ■ Kelbrook
- ■ Pilling
- ■ Trawden
- ■ Whalley

Leicestershire
- ■ Oakham

Lincolnshire
- ■ Alford
- ■ Bardney
- ■ Bassingham
- ■ Billingborough
- ■ Billinghay
- ■ Binbrook
- ■ Bourne
- ■ Caistor
- ■ Colsterworth
- ■ Donington
- ■ Heckington
- ●■ Holbeach
- ■ Horncastle
- ■ Louth
- ■ Mablethorpe
- ■ Market Deeping
- ■ Market Rasen
- ■ Metheringham
- ■ Scotter
- ●■ Skegness
- ■ Sleaford
- ● South Witham
- ■ Spilsby
- ■ Sutterton
- ● Sutton Bridge
- ■ Swineshead
- ■ Tetford
- ■ Wainfleet
- ■ Woodhall Spa
- ■ Wrangle

Norfolk
- ■ Attleborough
- ●■ Catfield
- ■ Cromer
- ■ Diss
- ■ Docking
- ■ Downham Market
- ■ East Dereham
- ■ Fakenham
- ■ Foulsham
- ■ Harleston
- ● Heacham
- ■ Holt
- ■ Hoverton
- ■ Hunstanton
- ■ Long Stratton
- ■ Martham
- ■ Melton Constable

Mundesley
- ■ Mundesley
- ■ N Pickenham
- ●■ N Walsham
- ■ Reepham
- ■ Sheringham
- ■ Snettisham
- ■ Stalham
- ■ Swaffham
- ■ Upwell/Outwell
- ■ Watton
- ■ Wells-next-the-Sea
- ■ Wiggenhall

Northamptonshire
- ■ Aldwincle
- ■ Desborough
- ■ Geddington
- ■ Kings Cliffe
- ■ Oundle
- ■ Thrapston
- ■ Woodford

Northumberland
- ■ Allendale
- ▲■ Alnwick
- ●■ Amble
- ■ Belford
- ■ Bellingham
- ■ Berwick-upon-Tweed
- ● Colwell
- ● Glanton
- ■ Hadston
- ■ Haltwhistle
- ■ Haydon Bridge
- ■ Hexham
- ■ Pegswood
- ■ Rothbury
- ■ Seahouses
- ■ Wooler

Nottinghamshire
- ■ Collingham
- ●■ Sutton-on-Trent

Shropshire
- ■ Bishops Castle
- ■ Church Stretton
- ■ Clun
- ■ Craven Arms
- ■ Ditton Priors/Much
- ■ Wenlock
- ■ Ellesmere
- ■ Highley
- ■ Ludlow
- ■ Market Drayton
- ■ Maes-Y-Clawdd
- ■ Newport
- ■ Oswestry
- ■ Whitchurch

Somerset
- ■ Cheddar
- ■ Dulverton
- ●■ Minehead
- ■ Williton
- ■ Wincanton
- ■ Wiveliscombe

Staffordshire
- ■ Biddulph
- ■ Ellastone
- ■ Ipstones
- ■ Leek
- ■ Longnor
- ■ Rushton Spencer
- ■ Warslow
- ■ Waterhouses

Suffolk
- ■ Brome
- ■ Bungay
- ●■ Eye
- ■ Fressingfield
- ■ Halesworth
- ■ Laxfield
- ■ Leiston
- ■ Reydon
- ● Saxmundham
- ■ Stradbroke
- ■ Yoxford

East Sussex
- ■ Heathfield
- ■ Rye Harbour

Tyne & Wear
- ● Backworth

Warwickshire
- ● Church Lawford

Wiltshire
- ● Calne
- ■ Mere
- ■ Tisbury

N Yorkshire
- ● Askrigg
- ■ Burniston
- ■ Castleton
- ■ Easingwold
- ■ Filey
- ■ Gargrave
- ■ Hawes
- ■ High Bentham
- ■ Hinderwell
- ■ Hunmanby
- ■ Ingleton
- ■ Kirkby Malzeard
- ■ Kirkbymoorside
- ■ Leeming Bar
- ■ Leyburn
- ■ Long Preston/
- Hellifield
- ●■ Malton
- ■ Masham
- ■ Northallerton
- ■ Pateley Bridge
- ●■ Pickering
- ■ Reeth
- ● Richmond
- ■ Rippon
- ● Rosedale Abbey
- ■ Settle
- ■ Sheriff Hutton
- ■ Snainton
- ■ Staithes
- ■ Walkerville

S Yorkshire
- ● Dinnington
- ■ Thorne
- ● Wentworth

W Yorkshire
- ● Hebden Bridge
- ● Luddenfoo
- ● Marsden
- ● Ryhill
- ● Slaithwaite
- ●■ Todmorden

107

● 50/50 partnership scheme   ■ 100% funded factories   ▲ special schemes of industrial premises, either wholly financed by the Commission or financed in equal shares with local authorities. The factory programme which had started in 1974 had continued to grow such that by 1985, a year after the RDAs had come into operation, there had been over 900 factories completed in around 400 locations, mostly within the RDAs (Fig. 11.1 and Table 11.1), and managed for the Commission by English Estates.

The Rural Development Areas and their associated programmes were more than a new name for the Commission's priority areas for factory development. The wider brief given under the 1983 legislation and the requirement that each Rural Development Area should produce an integrated and cohesive development strategy (rather than just a building programme) meant that the Commission increasingly worked with a wider range of organisations, both public and private. Of course the old partnerships with local authorities and the Rural Community Councils continued but new arrangements became possible, for example with housing associations, training organisations, local enterprise trusts and the tourist boards.

Thus the Commission became involved directly with areas of rural policy with which it had previously not been able to engage. A major area in this regard was rural housing, which had emerged as a problem towards the end of the 1970s. A modest start was made in developing a 'craft homes initiative', where housing was linked to working space for rural craft workers. On a wider front, the Commission negotiated with the Housing Corporation to provide a topping-up scheme to meet the extra costs of building new houses in rural areas. The representations of the Commission and other organisations about the severity of rural housing need led eventually to the Corporation making separate allocations, albeit at a modest level, for rural housing. Support was also given to the provision of affordable housing through partnership with the National Agricultural Centre Rural Trust.

Rural transport was another area where the Commission sought to expand its activities. The Department of Transport was persuaded to provide an annual fund which was administered by the Commission to support innovative, often community-based, transport schemes. Rural Transport Advisers were also supported through CoSIRA. Tourism, too, came on the agenda, both at the local level in the Rural Development Areas (for example in providing funds for building conversions for tourism purposes) and at a broader level in a partnership with the English Tourist Board to develop rural tourism strategies for some areas. Tourism was also supported because of its importance in farm diversification. The Ministry of Agriculture traditionally had a narrow, farming-based, vision of the rural economy, but during the 1980s it was gradually persuaded, not least by the Development Commission, to take a wider view. The Commission played an important part in the government's Farming and Rural Enterprise Initiative, producing a widely-distributed booklet, *Action for Rural Enterprise*, which indicated the range of assistance available to rural businesses, not least its own services available through CoSIRA.

Rural at last

The 1983 Act had formally created a Commission where before there had technically been just a Development Fund and a group of Commissioners. Curiously, the opportunity was not taken at the time to identify the new body clearly with its rural context. While the other countryside agencies were evidently linked to their area of operations (countryside, nature), the Commission remained simply about 'development'. Moreover, empowering the Commission to take executive action had raised a question about the justification for retaining CoSIRA as a separate executive arm. CoSIRA activities had continued to grow during the 1980s. In addition to providing advice and training to manufacturing businesses, it had widened its portfolio to encompass tourist enterprises and advice to village shops. An analysis of those firms 'on the books' towards the end of the decade shows the diversity of enterprises which were then covered (Table 11.2).

Table 11.2 Small firms advised by CoSIRA's Business Service, 1987/88

Activity	% of client base	Average number of employees
Engineering	11.1	6.5
Plastics	1.9	8.5
Electrical/electronics	3.5	6.2
Vehicles	9.8	4.1
Garments/fabrics	3.8	7.0
Building	4.7	5.7
Wood	11.7	3.9
Crafts	13.6	2.3
Food & drink	4.7	5.3
Printing	3.3	4.0
Domestic manufacturing	2.3	4.3
Services	11.6	2.8
Leisure/tourism	7.4	2.5
Property developers/landowners	5.4	1.6
Miscellaneous	5.2	4.7
Total/average	**100.0**	**4.1**

(SOURCE: ANNUAL REPORT OF THE RURAL DEVELOPMENT COMMISSION, 1987/88)

Craft and related industries still accounted perhaps for a quarter of the portfolio, but the rest was made up of firms involved with modern manufacturing processes, including those with a 'high technology' element. Services and businesses involved with leisure and tourism made up nearly one in five of the total client base. And this base was by no means restricted to the new priority areas. Indeed, of some 32,000 clients advised in the year 1987/88, nearly two in three were to be found outside the RDAs. The changes which had taken place in recent years in the nature of the work done for small firms by the Development Commission's 'economic arm' was also evident from the type of advice which firms were requesting. Technical advice regarding the craft industries, such as thatching, saddlery and iron work, which had been the backbone of the old Rural Industries Bureau, made up a minuscule proportion of the work load. In the year 1988/89 just sixty-seven visits to thatchers were made by business advisers. In real contrast the equivalent figures for management accounting was 3,891, for building 2,781 and for marketing 1,910.

CoSIRA had, within a relatively short time and after some early teething troubles, developed an increasingly prominent national profile and had become well known, even beyond its immediate clients. It remained a separate company limited by guarantee with its own Board of Directors. With the opening of the new CoSIRA headquarters in Salisbury in 1980, the links between the Commission and its main 'agent' became less clear in the minds of those who were unaware of CoSIRA's origins and parentage. Small matters, such as the publication of separate annual reports, did not help to unify the two organisations.

CoSIRA campaign at Tideswell, Derbyshire, in 1978

An attempt to strengthen the links between the Commission and CoSIRA was made in October 1980, when Nigel Vinson took over the chairmanship of CoSIRA from Clive Wilkinson. Vinson in time gave way, in November 1982, to Mr David Davenport, who was also a Development Commissioner. These formal links at the Commissioner/Director level were only partly successful in closing what some perceived as a widening gap between the two organisations. CoSIRA had, understandably, developed its own culture as an organisation, and staff loyalty perhaps focused more towards Salisbury than towards the London headquarters of the Commission in Cowley Street.

CoSIRA, and its predecessor the Rural Industries Bureau, had of course been formed simply because the original legislation which created the Commission had specifically prevented it from taking an executive role and dealing directly with private firms. The passing of the 1983 Act gave that executive authority to the Commission and thereby effectively removed the need for a separate agency. It followed, also, that there was a duplication of systems which, with the Commission's own staff increasingly getting involved on the ground in the Rural Development Areas, could lead to confusion. There was clearly a need for some restructuring to match the new ways of working. A merger of CoSIRA with its parent, the Development Commission, was therefore effected in April 1988. The *Farm Land and Rural Development Act* of that year allowed the number of Commissioners to increase to twelve and four former Directors of CoSIRA became Development Commissioners. The organisation was restructured into three directorates, with policy work and responsibility for workspace and Rural Development Programmes remaining at the London headquarters in Cowley Street and other work operating from Salisbury. More authority for day-to-day operations was given to those responsible for programme delivery, while members of headquarters staff were able to concentrate more on the development of policy and the provision of advice to government.

The merger also provided the opportunity, if somewhat late in the day, for the Commission to amend its public name. In the three or four years previously the Commission had gradually moved towards a clearer statement of its function through its name, proclaiming itself at last as 'England's Rural Development Agency' and then, somewhat coyly, calling itself the Development Commission for Rural England, even though that name had no statutory basis. In 1988 the Rural Development Commission, complete with the mandatory logo, formally came into being, providing a clarification which, it might be argued, was nearly eighty years overdue.

Action for rural communities

The economic sector was not the only one which underwent radical change during the 1980s and the Commission brought in new arrangements in the delivery of its social and community programmes. At one level the general thrust stayed constant. The Rural Community Councils remained as major delivery agents of the social programme, with the network of Councils eventually becoming complete in its national coverage, through the creation of new Councils in Norfolk and the Isle of Wight. The Commission also continued to support the rural work of the

National Council for Voluntary Organisations, especially as it involved the support of the Rural Community Councils, and also that of the National Federation of Women's Institutes. All three elements had thus been in place for more than seventy years. In addition to these long-standing partners, the Commission also began to work with new organisations as was happening in the economic sphere. A specific example was a programme to provide advice to rural dwellers in which the Commission worked with the National Association of Citizens Advice Bureaux.

The decade was also to see major changes in the relationship between the Rural Community Councils and the Commission. In part these changes came about because of extraneous influences. The Conservative government, while apparently keen to support voluntary activity, was even more concerned to ensure accountability in public expenditure. Thus the Rural Community Councils increasingly found themselves in a position where their funding from the Commission had to be fully justified as to its purpose, to the point where eventually formal contracts for specific elements of work would be introduced.

But the pressures for change were also internal to the system. The staffing of the Rural Community Councils had begun to change over the years and with it there occurred an inevitable change of attitude. Historically, the Chief Officers of the Councils had frequently been found from the ranks of retired armed service officers and this had inevitably imbued them with a particular ethos. In the 1970s this had begun to change as rural community development began, albeit slowly, to gain a professionalism which had previously only been found in urban social work. The new field officer posts also served to encourage this development and this was reinforced when some of these appointments graduated to more senior positions. And, as noted earlier, there had been a change to a more activist role within the Rural Department of the National Council for Voluntary Organisations.

The creation of the Standing Conference of Rural Community Councils in the early 1970s had begun the drawing together of the individual Rural Community Councils into a loose network, which began to show the advantages of concerted action. A movement developed in the early 1980s, looking to a more unified national presence for the Rural Community Councils. To some extent this had been provided by the creation of Rural Voice, particularly as the Standing Conference provided the secretariat for the new lobby group through the services of the Rural Department of the National Council. But many in the Rural Community Councils wanted greater independence as the voice of rural communities.

Whilst there were some, both officers and members, within the Rural Community Councils who were wary of the moves towards creating a new organisation, the Commission, and particularly its Chairman, were apprehensive of Rural Community Councils becoming more of a campaigning force. The main obstacle to independence was the National Council of Social Service. It had been funded by the Commission since the 1920s, primarily to support Rural Community Councils. By the mid-1980s the grant to the National Council from the Development Commission was in excess of £250,000 – a significant sum, especially at a time when other sources of funding were dwindling and the National Council's finances were far from healthy. The National Council was strongly opposed to the idea of an independent organisation for the Rural Community Councils and argued that the existing arrangement, involving themselves and the Standing Conference, was an entirely satisfactory one. The situation was given a certain piquancy by the fact that the National Council's own Chief Rural Officer, David Clark, was a prime mover in the call for independence. While he argued with justification that he and his team were simply reflecting the wishes of the Rural Community Councils, it must nevertheless be recognised that the movement to independence would have been stillborn had he taken a more passive role.

In the July 1984 policy statement, *The Next Ten Years*, the Development Commission had recognised the new activity in the Rural Community Councils and had specifically raised the question of whether they 'needed strengthening or greater freedom of operation'. To answer the question, and also to resolve the difficulties which were noted above, one of the Development Commissioners, Alan Leavett, was asked to conduct an enquiry into the role and relationships of Rural Community Councils and to make recommendations. It was, in fact, barely ten years since Brian Lincoln had conducted the last such review. His conclusions then were broadly that the existing arrangements should remain. But the world had changed very substantially in the intervening years and it seemed most unlikely that Leavett would also favour the *status quo*.

Reflecting the new pro-active spirit, the Standing Conference embarked on its own review in parallel to the Leavett enquiry. An intense period of lobbying, discussion and information exchange followed, during which feelings on all sides were often high. The National Council, under its formidable Chairman, Peter Jay, was obviously loath to lose the valuable link with the Commission, and it argued that a new, more independent Standing Conference would, away from the protective umbrella of the National Council, in fact be less independent and would end up as 'a potentially paternalistic centralised body, tied to the DC, and undermining the independence of RCCs'. On the other hand, the Rural Community Councils had an understandably strong 'adolescent' wish to go their own way. The new directions which rural community work had taken in recent years had inspired them to stand on their own feet. They wanted their own bargaining position and not one which, whether involving the distribution of resources or the ability to comment publicly on important issues, had always to be mediated through the National Council.

Leavett had previously had a successful career in the Civil Service, latterly in the rural section of the Department of the Environment. He brought to his investigation a deep and intelligent knowledge of the issues, coupled with years of experience in dealing with intractable situations. His report appeared in May 1985. It broadly supported the aspirations of the Rural Community Councils to take responsibility for their own development, though it was properly critical of some aspects of their performance which would have to be improved. It recommended further that the Development Commission should continue to fund the National Council to provide an 'intelligence unit', though the level of funding would inevitably be much lower than before. While the Leavett Report only provided a framework for future relationships, and much had still to be decided, it did deliver what was needed – an informed, balanced and authoritative assessment upon which new foundations for the Development Commission's rural social work could be built.

It was a measure of the quality of Leavett's analysis that all sides effectively accepted his findings and embarked upon a period of negotiation to decide the detail of the new structural relationships. A 'concord' group was formed between the Standing Conference and the National Council, which presented its proposals to the Commission in August 1986. As Leavett had intimated, a new organisation, independent of the National Council, was to be formed, with a small rural unit remaining in the National Council. The following year the new organisation, Action with Communities in Rural England (ACRE), was formed with Dr Malcolm Moseley, a senior academic from the University of East Anglia, as its first Director.

Conclusion

The ten years of Lord Vinson's chairmanship were in their own way as eventful and full of action as those of his predecessor. In line with the spirit of the times, the size of the permanent staff of the Commission had changed relatively little over the decades. In 1981 thirty-five staff were employed directly by the Development Commission, while CoSIRA had a staff complement of 301. By 1989 the integrated Commission was employing just 347 staff. Yet the range and the quantity of work was much increased. A gross budget in 1981 of £16.8 million had grown to £38.6 million by the end of the decade. The portfolio of financed workshops had trebled in size over the same period to more than three million square feet of space while a similar increase had taken place in the number of small firms which were advised. The Commission's client list in 1989 was nearly 33,000, spread across a range of enterprises from the traditional manufacturing and service sectors to include village shops, tourism concerns and transport undertakings. Research and publication had also grown apace. In 1989 there were eighteen research projects which the Commission was funding and in the same year over twenty publications were issued.

On the social side, also, the Commission's work had expanded substantially. Funding for the traditional activities, the Rural Community Councils, the National Council for Voluntary Organisations and the National Federation of Women's Institutes continued, albeit under a new regime in relation to the first two. In addition, the Commission was directly supporting a range of activities, especially in the Rural Development Areas, including transport schemes, community centres, field officers and projects in the arts, sports, education, and advice. And, again as noted earlier, the Commission had moved from simply expressing a concern for rural housing issues to giving grants to voluntary bodies for housing work and to co-operation with the Housing Corporation on a specific rural housing programme.

Yet these quantitative measures of performance were perhaps less significant than were the constitutional and structural changes which took place. Most obviously the 1983 Act had changed the legislative basis of the Commission and had given it new powers and duties. Indeed it actually created a Commission where none had formally existed before. Secondly, the separate agency for

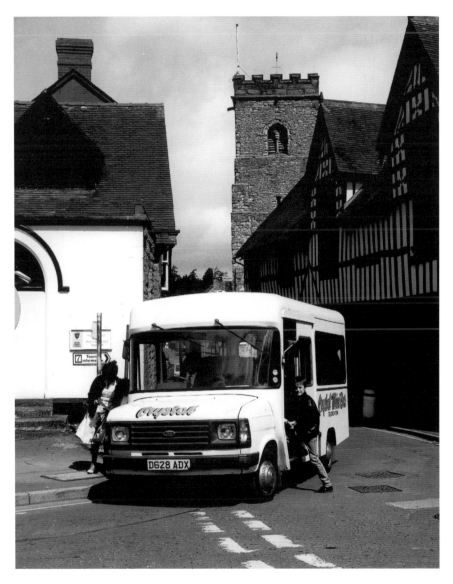

Crystal Mini Bus, grant-aided by the Commission, operating a route between Much Wenlock and Telford, Shropshire, in 1987

rural business advice and support, which had originated in the creation of the Rural Industries Intelligence Bureau back in 1921, was ended when CoSIRA was absorbed into the Rural Development Commission in 1988. And finally, the Rural Community Councils, which had been fostered by the National Council of Social Service since 1921, also achieved a new relationship with the Commission in 1987. All these developments, both quantitative and qualitative, had

resulted in the Rural Development Commission gaining a public reputation which was noticeably greater than at any time in its history. The scene was set for further growth, and even greater changes, in the next decade.

Signs of change at the Royal Show, Warwickshire, in 1988

CHAPTER 12

The ninth decade 1990–1999

It was clear from the previous chapter that during the 1980s the Rural Development Commission, while significantly increasing the range and quantity of its work, had also to adapt to a new political environment. The new situation continued into the 1990s, when Margaret Thatcher was replaced by John Major. Most obviously this was seen in the requirement that the Commission engage more with activities in the private sector. Significantly, however, new organisations, both public and private, were coming on the scene and were viewed as operating in many of the traditional arenas which had been pioneered by the Commission. At one level, this was simply a repetition of a process which had been continually present throughout the whole of the Commission's history. At another, it was to provide major challenges to the Commission staff and was, by the end of the decade, to have threatened its very existence.

A concomitant and growing problem for the Commission during the 1990s was financial pressure. The decade opened with two years of underspending by the Commission, due mainly to failures by the agents which built workspace for the Commission. The underspend inevitably weakened the case for increased funding and even for retaining current levels of resource. The Commission was also required to fund more of its activities by selling its portfolio of workspace – around £50 million of expenditure was financed in this way – which posed a threat to the level of its activities once these assets had been liquidated. In fact, before this point was reached the Commission was required to hand over its remaining workspace portfolio to the newly-founded English Partnerships on terms which meant, after a transitional period, that the Commission's income fell by £2 million a year.

These financial pressures had to be faced by a new combination of Chairman and Chief Executive. John Williams, who had worked with Lord Vinson for virtually the whole time of his chairmanship, retired in 1989. He was followed by Richard Butt, who had previously worked at the Treasury and with English Heritage. In turn, Lord Vinson retired in May 1990, to be replaced by Lord Shuttleworth. Charles Shuttleworth was, by training, a chartered surveyor who had been Chairman of the Lancashire Small Industries Committee since 1978. As the fifth Lord Shuttleworth he was, in fact, the great grandson of the Chairman of the inland waterways Royal Commission, which had reported in 1909 and which was referred to in Chapter 1. He came to the Commission with a specific interest and competence in the activities of rural businesses and a strong belief in the role of the Commission to support them. His commitment in this regard was to be sorely tested towards the end of the decade.

Lord Shuttleworth talking to hill farmers in Cumbria, 1991

New pressures in the countryside – and on the Commission

Financial pressures were not the only ones which the Commission had to tackle under its new leadership. Other problem areas in the countryside had emerged. A significant set of problems arose from declining employment in the coalfield areas. Since 1984 some 30,000 jobs had been lost in the English coalfields, with particular black spots being found in the East Midlands and South Yorkshire. Concern by the Commission for the coalfield problem had first arisen in the 1980s and some new work had been undertaken then. As time progressed, and further pits were closed, the problem grew worse. The Commission responded by a major programme of investment, allocating £6 million in the period 1990-1993, money which, in association with the local authorities, went towards creating workspace, giving business advice and improving local environments and social and community services. Parts of South Yorkshire, Nottinghamshire, Derbyshire and Leicestershire were designated as Rural Coalfield Areas and were able to benefit from the programmes which were available in the Rural Development Areas. The Commission also intensified its work in those rural coalfields which lay within the Rural Development Areas. The Commission's response was not just based upon its assessment of the social and economic stresses in these declining areas. It also reflected a wish to make clear to government that the agency was not just concerned with 'traditional' rural problems. On the contrary, it was very capable of handling the problems of decline in other rurally-based industries. A near-automatic acceptance of the value of the Commission's role by Conservative politicians in the past was often not shared by the new breed of Member of Parliament, and Minister, from the 1980s. Accordingly, the Coalfield Initiative, along with an equivalent endeavour in the china clay industry in Cornwall, was seen as an important proof of the Commission's continuing purpose.

The Commission also drew attention to some of the consequences of the so-called 'peace dividend'. The reductions in the armed services following the end of the Cold War led to problems, especially of unemployment and housing, in some rural areas where large service bases had been sited. Parts of the Rural Development Areas, especially in East Anglia and Lincolnshire were particularly affected.

Some of the pressures in the countryside to which the Commission responded were of a more traditional kind. Most notably there was concern about the radical changes taking place within agriculture. Declining employment in farming had been a constant theme in the life of the Commission since its foundation, but in the post-war period the Commission had had little direct involvement with agriculture. In part, this was because the farming industry was seen as the prime responsibility of the Ministry of Agriculture but it also reflected the comparative prosperity of agriculture in the years after the war. By the early 1990s, however, this situation had altered. Partly as a result of decisions emerging from the Uruguay Round of the General Agreement on Tariffs and Trade (GATT), changes were occurring in the Common Agricultural Policy of the European Union which were reducing farm price support. In the post-war world, farmers had generally received substantial support from government with the result that, while employed labour on farms had continued to decline, farm businesses as such had survived and even prospered. Now bankruptcy, reminiscent of the 1930s, had returned and with it the need to help remaining businesses to diversify and become more efficient.

The Commission responded to this problem in June 1991 by publishing a consultation paper, *Meeting the Challenge of Agricultural Adjustment*.

The report forecast job losses of up to 100,000 in farming and the ancillary industries in the 1990s and argued that some rural areas would find it very difficult to adjust to this. It proposed a new initiative with the result that, with government support, the Commission created a Countryside Employment Programme (CEP) as part of an overall government policy initiative called Action for the Countryside, which was launched in February 1992. Three pilot CEP areas were set up in Lincolnshire, the Cotswolds and the Marches, within which local partnerships, led by Commission staff, drew up strategies to improve farm incomes, encourage diversification in the manufacturing and service industries and improve the provision of training for those forced out of the traditional, land-based industries. By the end of the year 1994/95, when the scheme ended in the Marches and Lincolnshire (the Cotswold CEP continuing for a further year), some 200 projects had been jointly funded. The record of achievement in these areas was impressive, and included support for nearly 4,000 businesses, training provision for 13,000 people and an estimated total of 770 permanent jobs. The Countryside Employment Programme also provided some valuable lessons for the Commission about local rural development and it influenced the review of the Rural Development Programmes from 1994.

New, and old, ways of working

These new initiatives were not conceived in an *ad hoc* fashion but were part of a process of re-thinking, which the Commission undertook in the early 1990s. The review was prompted by the arrival of the Chief Executive, Richard Butt, and the new Chairman, Lord Shuttleworth, and by periodic questioning by the Treasury of the need for certain Commission activities, such as the provision of workspace. The conclusions of the various reviews, which were announced in December 1993, confirmed that the Commission would continue to target most of its resources on the development of the neediest rural areas, restricting its business services and workspace programmes entirely to these areas in future. At the same time, the Commission defined more clearly its other two main areas of work – national advisory work for government and others and countrywide action, particularly on rural service and deprivation. Practical manifestations of the new strategy included the introduction of a new initiative, Rural Challenge, to operate alongside Rural Development Programmes and to provide large-scale resources to a small number of major rural development projects. The Rural Challenge initiative had been proposed by the Department of the Environment and the Commission had accepted the proposal on the understanding that the cost, which would build up to £6 million a year, would be funded by new money. Second, several small programmes were combined in a new Policy Development Fund, with extra money to promote policy innovation demonstration projects and dissemination of good practice on rural issues.

Third, a review of Rural Development Areas and their associated Rural Development Programmes were announced. The Commission used the preceding review of the Rural Development Areas as the occasion to examine the case for maintaining rural priority areas and the targeting of programmes. It concluded that this approach was still valid and adopted the term 'rural regeneration' to cover the work done in priority areas, seeking, thereby, to gain for it comparable status and political profile with the 'urban regeneration' activities of other parts of government. The review of Rural Development Areas involved an intensive programme of data analysis and consultation, culminating in the announcement of the new areas in December 1993. The new RDAs (Fig.12.1), which were to come into force in April 1994, covered a slightly larger area of England than their predecessors, involving some twenty-nine counties and about one third of the area of the country. They incorporated the Rural Coalfield Areas and two of the pilot Countryside Employment Projects, which had been designated in the early 1990s. They also matched, to a considerable extent, the revised European Union rural priority areas (Objective 5b), designated in 1994 partly on the basis of data from the Commission.

Beyond the review of strategy, important managerial changes were also put in train. Since the merger with CoSIRA the Commission had maintained its two headquarters in Cowley Street, London and Castle Street, Salisbury. In practice, the London office was the base for staff involved with policy work and programmes, while the Salisbury office focused more upon the delivery of business support programmes in the field, as well as maintaining the Commission's technical expertise in crafts. The new Chief Executive was keen to integrate management of the different aspects of the Commission's work and to decentralise it and create a strong regional structure for the Commission. Accordingly, all operational programmes were concentrated in a single directorate and staff and responsibilities were transferred to new Regional Managers. From then on these managers were responsible for the delivery of all the Commission's main programmes and were the point of contact for local partners. Initially the regional structure was two-tier, with just four regions and nine area offices under them, a structure that was less than ideal due to government staffing restrictions. This was a source of duplication and in 1997 a more robust structure of seven single-tier regions was put in place. Following a review by Dame Anne Mueller, a Commissioner and former Permanent Secretary, the Commission's networked voluntary county committees was retained and, whilst losing all involvement in executive work, was given a stronger promotional and influencing role.

The Commission had, since its inception, developed a tradition of working in partnership with other organisations; indeed for most of its life it had seen itself as an enabler of other organisations' actions rather than an executive body in its own right. While the new statutory status created under the 1983 Act had changed this position, the Commission continued its tradition of partnership in the 1990s. While it continued to work with its traditional partners, such as the local authorities and the Rural Community Councils, it had also begun, from the 1980s, to co-operate more with the other countryside agencies, with bodies such as the Training and Enterprise Councils, the regional tourist boards, Business in the Community and with private companies.

This co-operation was energised by a number of governmental initiatives for rural areas, of

Fig. 12.1 Development Commission Rural Development Areas as designated in 1993

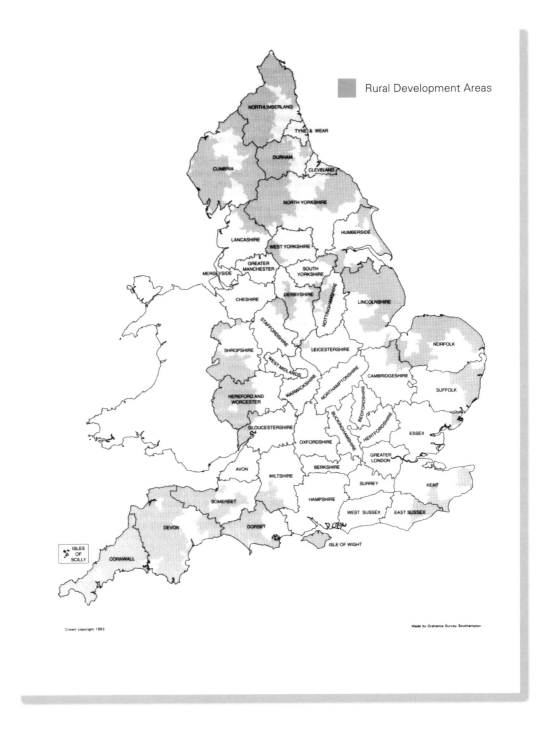

which the Commission was seen as a key part. The initiative Rural Action, launched in 1992, was designed to encourage voluntary activity to improve local environments and involved a partnership between the Commission and the other countryside agencies. By its third year of operation some 1,500 projects had been supported in forty counties, the majority of which were directly related to the Commission's own objectives in social and economic development.

A second initiative has already been mentioned. Rural Challenge extended into rural areas a governmental philosophy of competition for development funds, which had started in the urban areas. Commencing in February 1994, Rural Challenge created an annual competition for six prizes, each of £1 million, for major rural regeneration projects. Again, this initiative was seen to be based on the principle of partnership. The financial contribution from the Commission was expected to attract substantial resources from other sources and organisations involved with the particular projects. Finally the Commission became more involved with rural development activities emanating from Europe. In particular it co-ordinated two of the LEADER (Liaison Entre Actions de Dèveloppement de l'Economie Rurale) projects based in West and North Cornwall.

The increased level of activity on the part of the Commission and, more specifically, the growing amount of joint working and partnerships with other organisations, was in one sense, as noted before, simply a continuation of a *modus operandi* which had started in 1910. But in another sense it emphasised a paradox, for it raised in some minds the perennial question as to the specific role of the Commission itself beyond that of a provider of funds. If it linked with other organisations whose objectives, whether social, economic or environmental, were more narrowly focused, was it not running the risk of being seen as duplicating their work?

And this raised a second dilemma. In 1983 the Commission had at long last gained the executive status which had been denied it by Lloyd George all those years before. It proceeded to absorb its executive arm, CoSIRA, and 'do things for itself'. Yet at just this time the thrust of governmental opinion and policy was moving speedily away from government 'doing things' to facilitating others to do them. In practice, the governmental act of giving with one hand and taking with another was not immediate. It started when Lord Vinson was Chairman and continued under Lord Shuttleworth. It was he, his Commissioners and staff who would have to battle with the full consequences.

The Commission responded to these pressures by progressively seeking partnership projects with local authorities and others, by contracting out the development and management of its much reduced workspace programme and by outsourcing specialist business advice. Not all schemes to move from the Commission's traditional role of a provider of services to the preferred one of an enabler were, however, followed through. An attempt in 1994/95 to discontinue the provision of craft training in Salisbury and to transfer the operation to a mainline training provider, such as a further education college, ran into strong public criticism as well as proving financially unviable, and was dropped.

The policy and resource pressures of these years mainly affected the regeneration work of the Commission; the advisory work and the social programmes were less questioned by the government. During the decade, the responsibility which the Commission had to advise government on rural issues was followed through with increasing commitment, aided by the presence of Commissioners like Professor Howard Newby, Richard Best, (Director of the Rowntree Foundation), the Bishop of Dorchester and Dame Anne Mueller. Responses were made to consultation papers on topics as varied as the retail petrol market, housing and rural childcare. Advice was also given on a variety of planning matters and on the rural implications of proposals affecting the privatised utilities and the Post Office. Good practice guides were produced on rural enterprise, young people, childcare, village shops and rural transport.

The traditional links with the Rural Community Councils were maintained, not least because the Councils themselves became part of the local partnerships which took up the new initiatives like Rural Action, Rural Challenge and LEADER. A review of the Commission's 'Social Programme', carried out by Aston Business School and published in May 1991, was broadly supportive of the programme's achievements and value, though it did criticise some aspects of the work, which it felt had sometimes been insufficiently innovative. Significantly, the report supported the continuation of the arrangements which had been set up as a result of the Leavett Report, recommending continued funding of the Rural Community Council's federal body ACRE and of the Rural Unit in the National Council for Voluntary Organisations.

In many ways, however, the 1990s saw real changes in the ways in which the Commission's social programme was delivered and financed. The creation of ACRE had put the relationship between the Commission and the Rural Community Councils on a rather different footing. In the national policy arena the Commission had to get used to a more independent voice coming from the Rural Community Councils than had been the case before. And this independence extended to the negotiations over funding, which were now clearly the responsibility of ACRE and were no longer mediated through the National Council for Voluntary Organisations.

While the Commission accepted the main thrust of the Aston Report that funding of the Rural Community Councils should continue, it decided that such funding should move away from the traditional approach, which had provided core funding for 'general community work' since the early 1920s. In this it was joining the contract culture which had gradually pervaded more and more parts of public expenditure. Thus the Rural Community Councils, and indeed ACRE itself, had increasingly to gain its finance through the performance of agreed tasks. Eventually this process of change would be formalised in April 1995, when funding from the Commission to the Rural Community Councils was to come from 'service agreements', under which each Council undertook to deliver specified services locally under a number of standard headings.

Rural Community Councils were key partners in another new venture of the Commission, which focused on a long-standing concern – the loss of rural services. The evidence for service loss had always been rather patchy – a blend of partial statistics and anecdote, which nevertheless always managed to gain public attention. From 1991 the Commission attempted to put the evidence on a sounder footing. Enlisting the help of the Rural Community Councils and, through them, the clerks to parish councils, a national survey of rural services was carried out. This provided baseline data to be matched with subsequent national surveys in 1994 and 1997, data which was useful to government and others in dealing with rural policy.

The Commission had, early on in the decade, taken a conscious decision to expand its support for rural services and facilities. In some cases, such as the Rural Transport Development Fund, this entailed a broadening of the scope of the scheme and increases in the budget. In others it meant additions to programmes which were already established. This applied, for example, in the case of village halls. Overall support was increased and for three years the Commission operated a special programme to help with the extra costs of complying with new and more stringent health and safety requirements.

Particular attention was given to the question of affordable housing. Support for the Rural Housing Trust was continued for several more years. A new scheme to appoint rural housing 'enablers' was instituted. By 1994 these posts, which co-operated with local communities, landowners, local authorities and others to bring on housing schemes, existed in four counties, with a further ten posts under consideration. The problem of land availability was tackled by the creation of 'option land banks' from 1992. These schemes, which had been pioneered by the Community Council of Devon, encouraged landowners to promise small allocations of land at affordable prices which would be available as and when a local housing need was established. In 1996 a grant scheme was added to the existing advisory service for helping village shops.

The Rural White Paper

The Conservative government under John Major had, in the early 1990s, begun to show rather more interest in broad countryside policy than had its predecessor under Margaret Thatcher. As noted earlier, it had introduced new initiatives and schemes in the economic, social and environmental spheres which the Rural Development Commission had taken on board. This did not, however, mark a return to the traditional partiality which governments had often shown to the countryside, and particularly agriculture, in the past, a partiality from which the Commission had undoubtedly benefited. It was, in part, a response to powerful environmental pressure groups which successfully presented the landscape and wildlife resources of the countryside as being under serious threat from agriculture and development. But it also reflected a growing realisation by government, informed by Commission research, that the countryside also suffered from social and economic disadvantage. The balance of this governmental interest was undoubtedly environmental, encouraged by two 'green' Secretaries of State for the Environment – Chris Patten and John Gummer. However, there was recognition that countryside conservation went hand-in-hand with a healthy rural economy and the Commission was, therefore, able to extract from government an increased commitment to the countryside and some extra support for economic and social programmes.

At a broad level, this increasing significance of rural matters reflected the continuing movement of an articulate middle class to the countryside. At a narrower political level, it was clear that there were emerging particular tensions within government, not least between the relevant ministries in agriculture and in environment. Thus there had developed a public demand, but also a political imperative, for a comprehensive review of countryside policy.

Government responded to this situation by announcing, in October 1994, the intention of producing a White Paper on countryside policy, which would be written under the auspices of both the Ministry of Agriculture and the Department of the Environment. The White Paper was effectively the first major statement of national rural policy since the Scott Report of a half-century earlier. The contrast, as far as the Rural Development Commission was concerned, could hardly have been greater. Then, it will be remembered, the Commission had been consulted by the Scott Committee but had been laggard in its response. More seriously, it had totally misread the future importance of the Scott investigation and had, in consequence, received virtually no mention in the final Report. In the White Paper, published in October 1995 as *Rural England: a nation committed to a living countryside*, the Rural Development Commission contributed a substantial amount of statistical information as well as many examples of good practice in rural development, and was accorded prominent recognition for its past actions and future promise. Admittedly its endeavours were well attuned to the enthusiasms of the government – the commitment to fostering enterprise and economic growth, the involvement with partnerships and the equally long-standing association with the rural voluntary sector were all themes which were in common. The Rural White Paper appeared to offer the Rural Development Commission a major role in future rural policy, an impression reinforced by the first review of the White Paper which appeared in 1995.

The move to merger

This chapter began with a recognition of the financial pressures, which pressed in upon the Commission in its ninth decade. The requirement from government to do more with less had begun to appear in the 1980s, but it was in the 1990s that both staffing levels and financial resources were especially stretched. In part, the Rural Development Commission was simply being put under the same pressures as any other governmental agency, but in another way it appeared that the Commission was being specifically targeted by those who were critical of its purpose and covetous of its resources.

A precursor of troubles to come appeared in March 1994, when there was published a critical and tendentious article in *The Economist*. Thirty years before, the same journal had been quite complimentary of the Commission's work, concluding, if rather patronisingly, that 'one of Britain's odder public bodies may occasionally do some good'. This time the tone was very different. The words were in themselves contradictory, at once arguing that 'deep in the heart of the English countryside, socialism lives', yet concluding that the Commission provided 'terrific excuses for

Tories... to stuff rural voters with other peoples' cash'. But beyond the sarcasm and partiality of the piece there were being rehearsed themes which had already taken root in the minds of some members of the Conservative government. In part this reflected a return to a preoccupation which had stated in 1979, when Margaret Thatcher was first elected, the demand to cut down on the number of 'quangos'. But it also related to the desires of some ministers to push for a re-allocation of public moneys towards their own endeavours. Ironically, it was just at the time that the Rural Development Commission was about to be lauded in the Rural White paper that these pressures were intensified.

The attack on the Commission predominantly focused on its economic activities. The transfer of the Commission's remaining factory portfolio to English Partnerships had meant that the Commission had lost a valuable income stream. The Commission's financial resources were further weakened by cuts in successive public expenditure rounds from 1995. These led it to review its strategy early in 1996 and to decide to phase out the Loan Fund and its factory building programme, in order to deal with the looming funding shortfall and to enable it to give somewhat higher priority to its national advisory and rural services work. And finally there was a return, albeit in a new form, to a previous criticism within government of Commission activity – the place of its business advisory service within broader, urban-centred structures.

A national advisory service, Business Links, had been created in the early 1990s by the President of the Board of Trade, Michael Heseltine. By mid-decade Heseltine, now Deputy Prime Minister, was pressing for the new network to be strengthened by the absorption into it of the advisory services which came under other departments. The proposals were a direct threat to the independence of the Commission's business advisory service and its budget.

Commissioners responded as robustly as they could to these pressures. A compromise position was secured by the Secretary of State for the Environment, John Gummer, whereby it was agreed that the Commission's business service would remain separate but co-operate more closely with Business Links, and that part, but not all, of its budget would be transferred to a new competitive programme for Business Links – Local Challenge. The Commission, however, was under no illusion that this was but a temporary arrangement and that sooner or later its business services would be taken over. When the public expenditure settlement in autumn 1996 further reduced the Commission's budget, Commissioners decided in December that the Business Service would be closed down in the course of 1997/98. Thus ended a service to the rural business community which, in one form or another, had lasted for three-quarters of a century.

A new government – and yet more change

The election of the Blair government in May 1997 did nothing to lessen the pressures upon the Commission, even though in opposition it had professed itself committed to an active rural policy. The Labour Party had argued for a stronger regional dimension to government and planning and it was this commitment which was to present a new threat to the Commission. One aspect of this commitment when they came to power was reflected in the renaming of the Department of the Environment as the Department of the Environment, Transport and the Regions, under the control of the Deputy Prime Minister, John Prescott. There followed a consultation paper, setting out proposals to create Regional Development Agencies, which opened up the possibility that the Commission's regeneration work in rural areas would be subsumed into the new Agencies.

The Commission responded to the consultation paper by arguing strongly that the needs of rural areas, and the regeneration policies which should be implemented, were distinctive and that there was a real danger that a specific rural dimension within the new Regional Development Agencies would be overwhelmed by predominantly urban interests. A national body was necessary to champion the rural cause and to link at the grass roots level with its partners in rural development. Intense lobbying on behalf of the Commission seemed to have little effect in altering the direction of policy change, though the Minister of Agriculture, Jack Cunningham, spoke publicly in support of the Commission. Lord Shuttleworth decided to take a high profile stance on the issue and set out the Commission's operations publicly. However, in December 1997 John Prescott announced that the new Regional Development Agencies would incorporate the rural regeneration work of the Rural Development Commission. He also stated that government attached importance to maintaining the Commission's national advisory role and that he was reviewing, as a matter of urgency, the governmental organisations for delivering rural policy. Lord Shuttleworth concluded that he could 'not acquiesce in the break-up of an organisation, which has served rural England so well' and resigned immediately after Mr Prescott's statement. He was succeeded as Chairman by Miles Middleton, one of the existing Commissioners. Some months later the Commission's Chief Executive, Richard Butt, retired after nine productive if stressful years. His place was taken by John Edwards, who had been Director of Operations since 1995.

Finale – or pastures new?

In the event the Labour government took the decision not to destroy the Rural Development Commission in its entirety. In March 1998 it was announced that the Commission's work, national advisory function and its countrywide work would be joined with the Countryside Commission to create a new countryside agency to operate from April 1999. Subsequent decisions on public expenditure, following a comprehensive spending review, increased the budget for the new agency and thus gave some hopeful signs of its future effectiveness.

Throughout the nearly ninety years of its history, the Rural Development Commission weathered many storms and changes of policy. At times its survival seems, in retrospect, to have been little short of miraculous. In the 1930s, when urban unemployment was high and when public expenditure controls were strongly enforced, it could well have foundered. And again, after the Second World War, the Commission could well have gone under before Lady Albemarle took over as Chairman. Some would find it ironic that the latest and most serious challenge to its work has taken place after a quarter century of increased activity, during which time the need for broad-based rural development policies has become more widely recognised than at any time since the Commission's foundation. And there is perhaps a final irony in that the Commission, which had been so enthusiastically welcomed by Keir Hardie as 'the most revolutionary measure', and which had been revived after the Second World War with the specific help of Stafford Cripps, should be so radically altered by the descendants of their own Party.

Miles Middleton with children at the Early Years School, Bicker, Lincolnshire, 1998.
A redundant building grant from the Commission helped restore this village school,
which runs three nursery classes and provides education up to age eleven

APPENDIX A

The Rural Development Commission: a chronology

1909   Report of Royal Commission on the Poor Laws.

'People's Budget' speech by Lloyd George – mention of the Development Fund.

Development and Road Improvements Funds Bill introduced into Parliament (First Reading).

Second Reading of the Bill

Development and Road Improvement Funds Act (9 Ed. 7c. 47)

Creation of Development Fund with five Commissioners.

1910   General election – Liberals returned to power.

Debate on amendment to Act to increase number of Commissioners from five to ten. Eight eventually agreed.

Death of Edward VII.

Royal Warrant appointing eight Commissioners signed by George V and Winston Churchill.

First statutory meeting of the Development Commission.

First business meeting of the Development Commission.

Development and Road Improvement Fund Act (amendments).

Government of Ireland Act 1910 removes Northern Ireland from Development Commission sphere of activity.

1911   Research Institute in Plant Physiology created by Development Commission at Imperial College.

Cambridge Institute for Animal Nutrition created by Development Commission and attached to the School of Agriculture.

1912   Daniel Hall leaves Rothamsted to become a full-time Commissioner.

National Institute for Research in Dairying (NIRD) funded by Development Commission in collaboration with Board of Agriculture. Based at University College, Reading.

Plant Breeding Institute created by Development Commission at Cambridge.

Rowett Research Institute created by Development Commission in collaboration with Scottish Education Department.

1913   Approval by Development Commission of creation of Agricultural Economics Research Institute at Oxford by Ministry of Agriculture and Fisheries.

Horticulture Research Station created by Development Commission at East Malling in collaboration with South East Agricultural College, Wye.

Nursery and Market Garden Industries Development Society created in Lea Valley.

1914   Cheshunt (Hertfordshire) Station of Nursery and Market Garden Industries Development Society funded with help from Development Commission (later becoming the Glasshouse Crops Research Institute based at Littlehampton, Sussex).

1917   Survey for Ministry of Reconstruction advocating a central organisation to allocate funds etc. for rural industries.

1919   Appointment of an advisor on rural industries to the Development Commission.

            Development Commission provides £11,400 to help fund Welsh Plant Breeding Station.

            Creation of a Rural Department in the National Council of Social Service.

1920   Development Commission offers grant-aid of £10,000 to National Federation of Women's Institutes and £7,000 to Village Clubs Association for organisational work and creation of branches. National Federation of Women's Institutes grant operates until 1927.

            Oxford Conference of the National Council of Social Service, paving the way for the creation of the first Rural Community Council.

1921   Development Commission provides funds to National Federation of Women's Institutes for training in handicrafts (embroidery, basket making, quilting).

            Report on *Industries in Rural Districts* by Mr E C Kny.

            Development Commission creates Rural Industries Intelligence Bureau (RIIB).

            Country Industries Co-operative Society Ltd established to supply materials to ruralcraftsmen and to market products.

            First Rural Community Council founded in Oxfordshire.

1923   Second Rural Community Council founded in Kent.

            Grant from Development Commission to establish a Horticultural Research Station at Cambridge (eventually incorporated with Wellesbourne, Warwickshire in 1949).

            Rural Industries Intelligence Bureau name changed to Rural Industries Bureau (RIB).

            County federations of Women's Institutes in all English counties.

1924   Appointment by the RIB of a 'travelling representative' and the institution of a mobile welding demonstration van.

1925   Grant from Development Commission to Kent Rural Community Council to enable it to act as a local agent for rural industrial development.

            Rural Industries Bureau produced first edition of quarterly magazine *Rural Industries*.

            Review of progress regarding Village Clubs Association. Development Commission decides on no future funding.

            Development Commission adopts scheme whereby grant of £5,000 given to National Council of Social Service, for use through Rural Community Councils to provide interest-free loans for village halls.

            Development Commission offers grant to Scottish Women's Rural Institutes (SWRI) for handicraft training.

1928   Hannah Dairy Research Institute founded with Development Commission help.

            Rural Industries Bureau introduces quilting schemes in South Wales and Durham to provide home employment.

            Scottish Sub-Committee of Rural Industries Bureau established in Edinburgh.

            Development Commission takes over responsibility for financial assistance to SWRI from Board of Agriculture for Scotland.

1929   Development Commission funding Rural Community Councils in eleven counties.

            Development Commission provides funds for the Provisional Council for Welsh Rural Development to help rural industries in Monmouth, Glamorgan, Brecon and Radnor.

Development Commission extends scheme for village hall building. Further advance of £20,000 agreed. Scheme operates in counties with a Rural Community Council (fifteen) and by *ad hoc* committees in other counties.

Carnegie Trust adopts scheme to help village halls with supplementary grants to Development Commission aid.

1931   Expansion of work of Rural Industries Bureau – technical experts for craft trades.

Creation of the Agricultural Research Council.

1933   Development Commission increases grant to Rural Industries Bureau to £7,000 per year for 1933/34.

Development Commission aid to Society of Friends to encourage allotment provision and use especially in depressed areas.

1934   End of funding by Carnegie Trust to found Rural Community Councils. Rural Community Councils exist in twenty counties.

1936   Scottish Country Industries Development Trust (SCIDT) created (following 1933 Scottish National Development Council Committee). Development Commission gives grant of £1,600 for first year.

1937   End of establishment grants for RCCs from the Carnegie UK Trust. Role effectively taken over by the Development Commission.

1940   Rural Industries Equipment Loan Fund (RIELF) created (part of general war effort). Initially administered directly by National Council of Social Service (NCSS).

Headquarters of Rural Industries Bureau moved to Taunton, Somerset.

1944   Headquarters of Rural Industries Bureau moved from Taunton to Wimbledon.

1944/45   Discussions with National Council of Social Service regarding provision of village halls after the war. Eventual government agreement for provision of temporary village halls – 200 in England and Wales; 100 (later eighty-five) in Scotland. Scheme continued to 1965.

1945/46   Three-year commitment to core fund established Rural Community Councils – seen as an important contribution to post-war reconstruction.

1946   Death of Lord Richard Cavendish; Lord Shaftesbury appointed Chairman.

Development Commission relinquishes responsibility for agricultural research to Agricultural Research Council (administrative services provided until 1950).

1947   Rural Industries Loan Fund Society Ltd created, taking over from RIELF (1940). Administrative services provided by the NCSS; George Haynes acting as Chairman.

Workshops Loan Fund created.

Development Commission authorises loans to local authorities and other non-profit organisations to build advance factories. Factory programme starts in Wales and Scotland.

1948   Lady Albemarle becomes Chairman of Development Commission.

1950/52   Development Commission carries out comprehensive review of Rural Community Councils.

1952   Development Commission gains Treasury's agreement to make annual grants to RCCs until 1959.

1955   Development Commission relinquishes responsibility for funding construction and improvement of fishery harbours.

1959   Review of work of RCCs to decide on future of the block grant system. Block grants renewed for a further five years from April 1961.

1963 Working Capital Loan Fund created by RIB.

     Commissioners send a letter to the Prime Minister urging a re-assessment of rural policy.

1964 *Industrial Training Act 1964* takes over some of the RIB training and apprenticeship schemes.

     Mr F.S.O. Broughton retires as Secretary; succeeded by Mr B.E. Lincoln.

     Paper by Development Commission (*Prospects for rural development and re-development*) submitted to Prime Minister, arguing case for more co-ordinated rural policy. Proposal for Trigger Areas and expansion of general activities. Internal report, following review of RIB, on *Report on the effects of national planning on the functions and sphere of influence of the Rural Industries Service* – prelude to creation of CoSIRA.

1965 'Favourable' letter from Prime Minister in response to Development Commission paper.

     National Council of Social Service Village Hall Committee scheme continues with providing permanent village halls (grant from Department of Education and Science, Scottish Education Department and Development Commission funding).

     Development Commission relinquishes responsibility for fisheries research to newly-formed Natural Environment Research Council (following *Science and Technology Act, 1965*).

     Highlands and Islands Development (Scotland) Act, 1965. Development Commission work in Scotland thereafter largely restricted to areas outside Crofting Counties.

1966 *Industrial Development Act, 1966.* Designated wider Development Areas.

     Rural Industries Loan Fund moves to its own premises from the NCSS prior to creation of CoSIRA.

     Creation of Eastern Borders Development Association, fifty per cent funded by Development Commission.

1968 Registration of CoSIRA as a limited company.

     Creation of Council for Small Industries in Rural Areas (CoSIRA) [England and Wales] taking over Rural Industries Bureau (which becomes Advisory Services Division), work of RIOs (employed by Rural Community Councils) and Rural Industries Loan Fund (which becomes Credit Services Division). Tourism Loan Fund added.

1969 Creation of Small Industries Council for Rural Areas of Scotland (SICRAS) taking over functions of Scottish Country Industries Development Trust and the former Scottish Committee of the Rural Industries Loan Fund.

     Study of Rural Community Councils' work in England and Wales by Mr R. F. Bretherton recommending continued grant aid and expansion.

     Development Commission funds three experimental studies to look at problems of rapidly expanding rural communities in Hampshire, Cumberland and Monmouthshire.

     Field Staff Division of CoSIRA created from former Rural Industries Organisers employed by RCCs.

1970 Report on Development Commission activity in Mid-Wales by University College, Aberystwyth, concentrating on social and economic effects of factory building programme (published 1972).

     Former Rural Industries Committees in counties reconstituted as Small Industries Committees of CoSIRA.

     Issue of Bretherton Report on RCCs.

     Creation of Standing Conference of Rural Community Councils under NCSS auspices.

     Second memorandum from Development Commission to Prime Minister.

1971   Department of Environment assumes sponsorship of Development Commission from Treasury.

Report by R.H. Tann on the effectiveness of the advisory and credit services of CoSIRA. Work of CoSIRA field staff was scrutinised internally.

Report of Bolton Committee on Small Firms (set up in 1969) – favourable comments on work of Council for Small Industries in Rural Areas.

1972   Development Committee provides funds for 'community initiative officers' in Rural Community Councils – at first in a few Rural Community Councils on a three-year trial. Special concern given to environmental matters, liaison with emerging voluntary bodies etc.

1974   Lady Albemarle retires as Chairman; succeeded by Mr Donald Chapman (later Lord Northfield).

Report on rapidly expanding rural communities in Cumbria.

Rowntree Memorial Trust sets up Wolfenden Committee on voluntary organisations.

Mr B. Lincoln retires as Secretary; succeeded by Mr K.J. Reeves.

1975   Development Commission headquarters administration moved to Salisbury from Cowley Street, London.

Creation of Special Investment Areas, superseding the Trigger Areas.

New remit given by Government to the Development Commission.

Small Industries Council for Rural Areas of Scotland (SICRAS) becomes part of new Scottish Development Agency.

Initial sixteen 'countryside officer' schemes extended for further two years, 100 per cent funded by Development Committee. Further ten schemes approved.

Report on rapidly expanding rural communities in Hampshire.

Lincoln Report on Development Commission social programme.

1976   Report on Council for Small Industries in Rural Areas by Walter Lane published. Working Party of three Commissioners set up.

Creation of Welsh Development Agency – Wales removed from Development Commission's remit.

Publication of Inter-departmental Study on Rural Depopulation.

Working Party on Lane Report, report back to Development Commission.

1977   Social and community work in Wales and Scotland transferred to Scottish and Welsh offices.

Cllr Clive Wilkinson takes over as Chairman of Council for Small Industries in Rural Areas.

Proposal from Wilson Committee to merge Council for Small Industries in Rural Areas into English Development Agency.

Report of Wolfenden Committee on voluntary organisations published.

1978   Development Commission's first involvement with housing. Discussions with Housing Corporation.

Start of building of Council for Small Industries in Rural Areas headquarters in Salisbury.

Development Commission allowed greater funding freedom from DoE.

Publication of *The decline of rural services* report by Standing Conference of Rural Community Councils.

1979   Inter-departmental Government review of Development Commission and Council for Small Industries in Rural Areas (result 1982).

1980   Salisbury headquarters/workshops opened.

Mr Nigel Vinson succeeds Lord Northfield as Chairman of Development Commission.

Creation of Rural Voice.

Clive Wilkinson gives up chairmanship of Council for Small Industries in Rural Areas; succeeded by Nigel Vinson (later Lord Vinson).

1981   Management of factory programme outside Assisted Areas transferred from Council for Small Industries in Rural Areas to English Industrial Estates Corporation (later called English Estates) which already dealt with development in Assisted Areas.

Introduction of 'Pockets of Need' – problem areas outside Special Investment Areas.

Mr Kenneth Reeves retires as Chief Executive; succeeded by Mr John Williams.

Workshop programme – fifty/fifty with local authorities.

1982   Publication of Government Review (from 1979). Greater freedom of operation. Outline criteria for new Rural Development Areas.

Grant scheme for redundant buildings conversion, operated by Council for Small Industries in Rural Areas. Two year experimental period in some L.F.A s – then extended to all S.I.A.s (first time grants offered to individuals).

Government review of relationship between Council for Small Industries in Rural Areas and Department of Industry Small Firms Service. Against merger – activities seen as complementary.

Mr David Davenport appointed as Chairman of Council for Small Industries in Rural Areas.

Miscellaneous Financial Provisions Bill introduced into the Commons by John Wakeham.

1983   *Miscellaneous Financial Provisions Act 1983* passed (in force 1 April 1984) updating statutory basis of Development Commission (replacing Acts of 1909 and 1910). Development Commission now a grant-in-aid body.

1984   Publication of *The next ten years*.

New Rural Development Areas announced.

Reception to mark Development Commission's seventy-fifth anniversary.

1985   Report by Mr Alan Leavett - *Review of Rural Community Councils*.

1986   Launch of Rural Transport Development Fund.

'Concord' group (SCRCC and NCVO) submit proposals to Development Commission re ACRE.

Summary report on rural deprivation research published by Department of the Environment.

Establishment of Social Advisory Panel and Rural Training Advisory Panel.

1987   Foundation of Action with Communities in Rural England (ACRE).

Launch of ACCORD (Assistance for Co-ordinated Rural Development) Scheme.

Start of direct funding of ACRE by Development Commission.

National Conference on 'What Future for Rural Communities'.

1988   Farmland and Rural Development Act. Number of Commissioners increased to twelve.

Development Commission merges with Council for Small Industries in Rural Areas.

Government papers on housing in rural areas and new villages.

1989   Mr John Williams retires as Chief Executive; succeeded by Mr Richard Butt.

1990   Lord Vinson retires as Chairman; succeeded by Lord Shuttleworth.

1991   Publication of Aston Business School Report on *Managing Social and Community Development Programmes in Rural Areas* (evaluation of RDC Social Programme).

1992   Countryside Employment Programme (CEP) scheme launched as part of government's Action for the Countryside Initiative.

1993   Development Commission joins with Countryside Commission and English Nature to launch Rural Action.

Strategic review of Rural Development Commission.

New Rural Development Areas announced (in operation from 1 April 1994); publication of *The Future of the Rural Development Process*.

1994   Announcement by government of a Rural White Paper.

Launch of Rural Challenge.

1995   Funding for Rural Community Councils moves to service agreements.

Publication of government's Rural White Paper.

1996   Loan Fund and Business Advisory Service closed down.

1997   Proposal to create Regional Development Agencies.

1998   Decision by government to move regeneration work to the new Regional Development Agencies and to merge the remainder of the Rural Development Commission with the Countryside Commission.

Chairmen and Secretaries/Chief Executives of the (Rural) Development Commission 1910–1999

Chairmen

Lord Richard Cavendish	1910-1946
Lord Shaftesbury	1946-1948
The Countess of Albemarle	1948-1974
Mr D. Chapman (Lord Northfield)	1974-1980
Mr N. Vinson (Lord Vinson)	1980-1990
Lord Shuttleworth	1990-1997
Mr M. Middleton	1997-1999

Secretaries/Chief Executives

H.E. Dale	1910-1919
R.T. Warner	1919-1933
E.H.E. Havelock	1934-1955
F.S.O. Broughton	1955-1964
B.E. Lincoln	1964-1974
K.J. Reeves	1974-1981
J.V. Williams	1981-1989
R. Butt	1989-1998
J. Edwards	1998-1999

Sources

Published sources relating to the Rural Development Commission are few and far between – indeed that fact was a major spur to producing this history. This, and the need to produce a readable account have largely precluded much referencing in the text, though major reports and the like have of course been mentioned. This note concentrates on the key sources, other than personal interviews, which have been used in the production of this Report.

1. Published accounts

There are a number of 'histories of the countryside' which will provide the reader with valuable contextual information, even if specific references to the Rural Development Commission are limited. Gordon Mingay's magisterial *The Victorian Countryside* (two volumes, Routledge and Kegan Paul, 1981) is still the classic account of the condition of rural England at the outset of the period considered here. It has since been published in paperback and, together with some new chapters going into the twentieth century, has been republished in three separate volumes, all edited by Mingay – *The Rural Idyll, The Vanishing Countryman* and *The Unquiet Countryside* (Routledge, 1989). A good general account which is highly readable is Howard Newby's *Country life: a social history of rural England* (Weidenfeld and Nicolson, 1987). The early period covered by this Report is considered by Alun Howkins in *Reshaping rural England: a social history 1850-1925* (Harper Collins, 1991). A broad overview of twentieth century attempts to develop and plan the countryside can be found in *Rural change and planning: England and Wales in the Twentieth Century* (Spon, 1996) by Gordon Cherry and Alan Rogers.

Four publications which do consider the Development Commission in some detail are worthy of note. Jose Harris' *Unemployment and politics: a study in English social policy 1886-1914* (Clarendon Press, 1972) gives an excellent critical account of the foundation of the Commission. H.E. Dale, the first Secretary to the Commission, wrote a biography of Daniel Hall (*Daniel Hall: pioneer in scientific agriculture*, John Murray, 1956), in which he considers Hall's years at the Commission between 1910 and 1917 in some detail, if with a touch of sycophancy. Chris Minay, of Oxford Brookes University, is virtually alone in the academic community in having researched the Development Commission in recent years. See particularly his *The Development Commission's rural industrial development programme: a review of progress 1945-1985* (Oxford Polytechnic, Department of Town Planning Working Paper No. 87, 1985). Finally, the relationships between the Development Commission, the Rural Community Councils and the National Council of Social Service are reviewed, if rather uncritically, in Margaret Brasnett's *Voluntary social action: a history of the National Council of Social Service* (NCSS, 1969).

2. Publications of the Rural Development Commission

Annual Reports of the Development Commission were produced from 1911 to 1939. By today's standards they contain an amazing amount of meticulously-recorded detail. Thereafter, no Reports were made to government until 1961, when they reappeared, albeit sporadically, and covering a number of years at a time. Annual Reports were re-established in 1977.

From the 1920s there came a stream of reports, manuals and pamphlets, especially from the Rural Industries Bureau. These were continued by the RIB's successor, CoSIRA, and also after the amalgamation of CoSIRA into the Commission. The last twenty years have seen a positive flood of publications by the Commission, relating to particular schemes and initiatives which have been launched at various times; to major policy developments; and, in more recent years, to an impressive programme of research on key rural policy issues.

A history of the Rural Industries Bureau and of its successor, the Council for Small Industries in Rural Areas, was the subject of an unpublished study by Mr S.M. Algar, an employee of CoSIRA. While this study *(A history of CoSIRA 1909-1979)* contains some factual errors, it has been of real value in providing information on the rural industries work.

3. Public Record Office

Unpublished records of the Development Commission are to be found in the Public Record Office at Kew under the D-class listings. The Minutes of meetings (D1) are available from the twenty-ninth meeting held in November 1912, but the records of the first twenty-eight meetings are unfortunately lost.

Other records available at Kew include volumes and files of evidence relating to grant applications to the Development Fund (D2) and other internal reports, memoranda and notes on a wide range of topics (D4). The normal thirty-year rule applies regarding public access.

The Public Record Office reference number for the Post Office Telegraph reproduced in Chapter 2 is D4/950; for Fig. 3.1 it is D 3/3; and Figs. 4.1 and 4.2 are both D 3/10.

4. *Hansard*

Full reports on the debates and committee considerations in both Houses relating to the Acts of 1909, 1910, 1983 and 1988 can be found in *Hansard*.

Images used in this book

Pages 1, 5 © Rural History Centre, University of Reading

Page 12 Photographer and copyright unknown: Photograph taken from the Farmer and Stockbreeder, 6 May 1912

Pages 15, 51, 60, 75, 83, 91, 101, 110, 116 Photographer unknown /© RDC/Rural History Centre, University of Reading

Page 28 Photographer unknown. Photograph taken from the Rural Industries Bureau Report 1937-1947

Page 45 Front cover from the Rural Industries Journal, Autumn 1926

Page 46 Photographer unknown: © RDC/Rural History Centre, University of Reading

Page 86 © P. Newton/RDC

Page 115 © I. Forshaw/RDC

Page 118 © M. Hancock/RDC

Page 129 © B. Greenough/RDC

INDEX

INDEX

INDEX